U.S. Department
of Transportation

Research
Innovative
Technology
Administration

Assessment of Performance Measures for Security of the Maritime Transportation Network

Port Security Metrics: Proposed Measurement of Deterrence Capability

Prepared for:

Advanced Systems and Concepts Office
Defense Threat Reduction Agency
U.S. Department of Defense
8725 John J. Kingman Road, Fort Belvoir, VA

Prepared by:

U.S. Department of Transportation
Research and Innovative Technology Administration
John A. Volpe National Transportation Systems Center
Cambridge, Massachusetts
January, 2007

	Report Documentation Page		Form Approved OMB No. 0704-0188
	Public reporting burden for the collection of information is estimated to average 1 hour per response, including the time for reviewing instructions, searching existing data sources, gathering and maintaining the data needed, and completing and reviewing the collection of information. Send comments regarding this burden estimate or any other aspect of this collection of information, including suggestions for reducing this burden, to Washington Headquarters Services, Directorate for Information Operations and Reports, 1215 Jefferson Davis Highway, Suite 1204, Arlington VA 22202-4302. Respondents should be aware that notwithstanding any other provision of law, no person shall be subject to a penalty for failing to comply with a collection of information if it does not display a currently valid OMB control number.		
1. REPORT DATE 03 JAN 2007	2. REPORT TYPE N/A		3. DATES COVERED -
4. TITLE AND SUBTITLE Assessment of Performance Measures for Security of the Maritime Transportation Network, Port Security Metrics: Proposed Measurement of Deterrence Capability			5a. CONTRACT NUMBER
			5b. GRANT NUMBER
			5c. PROGRAM ELEMENT NUMBER
6. AUTHOR(S) Robert Hoaglund, CPP, Walter Gazda, PMP			5d. PROJECT NUMBER
			5e. TASK NUMBER
			5f. WORK UNIT NUMBER
7. PERFORMING ORGANIZATION NAME(S) AND ADDRESS(ES) U.S. Department of Transportation, Research Innovative Technology Administration, John A. Volge National Transportation Systems Center, 55 Broadway Cambridge, MA 02142			8. PERFORMING ORGANIZATION REPORT NUMBER
9. SPONSORING/MONITORING AGENCY NAME(S) AND ADDRESS(ES) Defense Threat Reduction Agency U.S. Department of Defense Fort Belvoir, VA 22060			10. SPONSOR/MONITOR'S ACRONYM(S)
			11. SPONSOR/MONITOR'S REPORT NUMBER(S)
12. DISTRIBUTION/AVAILABILITY STATEMENT Approved for public release, distribution unlimited			
13. SUPPLEMENTARY NOTES			
14. ABSTRACT			
15. SUBJECT TERMS			

16. SECURITY CLASSIFICATION OF:			17. LIMITATION OF ABSTRACT	18. NUMBER OF PAGES	19a. NAME OF RESPONSIBLE PERSON
a. REPORT unclassified	b. ABSTRACT unclassified	c. THIS PAGE unclassified	SAR	54	

Standard Form 298 (Rev. 8-98)
Prescribed by ANSI Std Z39-18

NOTICE

Neither the United States Government nor any agency thereof, nor any of their employees, makes any warranty, express or implied, or assumes any legal liability or responsibility for the accuracy, completeness, or use of any information, apparatus, product, or process disclosed. Reference herein to any specific commercial product, process, or service by trade name, trademark, manufacturer, or otherwise, does not necessarily constitute or imply its endorsement, recommendation, or favoring by the United States Government or any agency thereof. The views and opinions of authors expressed herein do not necessarily state or reflect those of the United State Government or any agency thereof.

DOCUMENT APPROVAL

Document Number of Final Version	Date of Document mm/dd/yyyy	Approver Initials	Date of Approval
Final (1.07)	01/03/2007		
Final draft (11.06)	12/08/2006	JG	12/08/2006
Final draft (11.06)	11/15/2006		
Draft (6.06)	09/14/2006	JG	09/14/2006
Draft (6.06)	06/30/2006		

DOCUMENT CHANGE HISTORY

Document Number	Version Number	Draft or final	Date of Document mm/dd/yyyy	Author's Initials	Author's Org	Description of Change
	11.06	Final draft	12/13/2006	RH	VNTSC	ASCO comments
	6.06	Draft	09/20/2006	RH	VNTSC	ASCO comments

TABLE OF CONTENTS

Section	Page
1. INTRODUCTION	1
1.1. Goal	2
1.2. The TVC Risk Paradigm	2
1.3. Overview of the Report	3
2. PERFORMANCE METRICS	4
2.1. Performance Measurement	4
2.2. Constructing Performance Measures	5
3. DETERRENCE	6
3.1. Risk Reduction	6
3.2. Views of Risk	7
3.3. Risk, Deterrence, and Ports	7
3.4. Crime and Criminal Behavior	7
3.5. Risk Biases	8
3.6. Risk Analysis and Deterrence	8
3.7. Handling the Problem of Risk	9
4. UNCERTAINTY AND POSSIBILITY THEORY	10
4.1. Problems with Probability	10
4.2. Approaches to Uncertainty	11
4.3. An Outline of the Theory of Evidence, Possibility Theory and Uncertainty	11
4.3.1. Possibility (Π) and Necessity (N)	12
4.3.2. Differences and Similarities between Possibility and Probability	12
4.3.3. Expressing Uncertainty and Confidence	13
4.3.4. How to solve the problem of measurement where there is insufficient data	14
4.3.5. Letting Go of Probability	14
4.4. Sample Possibility, Necessity and Uncertainty Calculations for the Interdiction Chain	15
5. APPLICATION TO MSRAM	20
5.1. An Approach to Adding Deterrence to MSRAM through Vulnerability	20
5.2. An Alternative Link between Probability and Possibility in MSRAM	21
5.3. Recommendations for Improving the MSRAM Process	22
5.3.1. Deterrence	22
5.3.2. An Iterative Process to Determine Possibility Using Experts' Judgment	23
5.3.3. Area Attacks	25
5.3.4. A Systems Approach	26
6. DEVELOPING ROBUST RISK ESTIMATES	27
6.1. Conceptual Maps	28
6.2. Ports as Complex Interacting Systems	28
6.3. Observable versus Unobservable Protection	29
6.4. The Use of Conceptual Maps	29
7. RECENT ADVANCES, FUTURE DIRECTIONS	35
7.1. Recent Advances	35
7.2. Recommendations with Respect to MSRAM	36
7.3. Adding Tipping Points and Non-Linearities to MSRAM	37

TABLE OF CONTENTS

Section	Page
APPENDIX A: OFFICE OF MANAGEMENT AND BUDGET'S (OMB'S) PERFORMANCE ASSESSMENT RATING TOOL (PART) PROCESS	38
APPENDIX B: ANALYTICAL HIERARCHY PROCESS	41
APPENDIX C: VERBAL EXPRESSIONS OF PROBABILITY	42
APPENDIX D: THE DELPHI TECHNIQUE APPLIED TO CREATING POSSIBILITY DISTRIBUTIONS	43
BIBLIOGRAPHY	45

LIST OF FIGURES

	Page
Figure 1: Triangular Distribution of Estimates of $\Pi(A)$	16
Figure 2: Sample possibility Distributions	17
Figure 3: Triangular Possibility Distribution of Arrival Time	19
Figure 4: Sample System Security Calculator Dialog Box	23
Figure 5: Conceptual Map of Deterrence Strategy	32
Figure 6: Simple Example of Driving Speed Determination	33
Figure 7: More Complex Driving Speed Decision Model	33
Figure 8: A Notional Example of the Influence of Deterrence on the Interdiction Chain	34
Figure 9: A Notional Example of the Influence of Investment on the Interdiction Chain, adding Deterrence and Interactions	34

1. INTRODUCTION

This report is the third in a series describing the development of performance measures pertaining to the security of the maritime transportation network (port security metrics). The development of measures to guide improvements in maritime security is particularly timely, as large sums of money are currently being devoted to security, while attempts to create meaningful performance-based indicators applicable to ports continue to present a challenge. Where measures do exist, it is important to continually refine them by refining assumptions to more accurately reflect the real world.

Ports and the surrounding harbor towns or cities where ships take on or discharge cargoes are composed of several facilities that serve as points of entry or departure for maritime cargo transport. As such, ports are a key component of the supply chain for both civilian and military cargo and personnel. Ports serve to maintain commerce and play a significant role in the nation's force projection capability. There are significant bottlenecks, however, since excess capacity is costly and the rail and road systems around ports are congested.[1] These factors make ports high value targets, as terrorist attacks on ports could result in the disruption of those activities. Further, terrorist use of ports as a transit point for weapons of mass destruction (WMD) and associated material could place the entire country and its population at grave risk.

This report focuses on issues related to the mission of the Defense Threat Reduction Agency's (DTRA) Advanced Systems and Concepts Office (ASCO), to

> Develop and maintain an evolving analytical vision of necessary and sufficient capabilities to protect the United States and allied forces and citizens from nuclear, biological, and chemical attack.[2]

An earlier report in this series described the legislative environment pertaining to maritime transportation security. The legislation was found to have resulted in a maritime security regime focused on performance-based goals rather than prescriptive ones, leaving wide discretion on the interpretation and implementation of security measures in each situation.[3] Another report in the series briefly characterized the significance of maritime commerce to both the US and world economies and then described the benefits of couching risk analyses in the context of the transportation network, in order to capture the consequences of disruptions.[4] This report represents a continuation of those earlier efforts and presents a contribution to the continual refinement of the Maritime Security Risk Analysis Model (MSRAM), the US Coast Guard's (USCG) principal analytic decision support tool for determining port risk.

---

[1] See, for example, Honea, "U.S. Military Preparedness – Jammed in the Traffic?," November-December, 2000.
[2] Taken from the DTRA ASCO website, www.dtra.mil .
[3] See, Volpe National Transportation Systems Center (a), *Port & Maritime Security Law Review*, Final Draft, December 2005.
[4] See, Volpe National Transportation Systems Center (b), *Port Security Metrics: Performance Measure Model Options*, Final Draft, January 2006.

1.1. Goal

The goal of this analysis is to provide ASCO and its customers with a comprehensive approach to the development of quantitative performance measures to assess security improvements to the port system and permit identification of existing security gaps. Such a capability will enable decision makers to assess, within a consistent framework, the merits of alternative security strategies and their subsequent implementation as investments in risk mitigation.

The uncertainty of the operating environment results in a need for robust planning methods. This, in turn, requires flexibility in the management of risk, evidenced here by the relaxing of some of the usual assumptions concerning risk determination. In describing the suggested approach to enhance some MSRAM functions, the analysis adheres to Office of Management and Budget (OMB) guidance, particularly with respect to the creation of performance measures and program governance as described in OMB's Program Assessment Rating Tool (PART) process. The application of some recent developments in decision science to port security problems, specifically in the context of deterrence, permits the incorporation of uncertainty into an analysis characterized by a lack of historical information and thus dependent upon expert judgment.

1.2. The TVC Risk Paradigm

Traditional risk assessment is exemplified by the "TVC" paradigm, with risk defined as the product of Threat, Vulnerability and Consequence. This is most often expressed as, literally, the arithmetic product of the three elements. This is the essence of the MSRAM methodology. The approach requires certain key assumptions and restrictions concerning, for example, the probabilistic interpretations of data, the independence of events, and linearity in decision-making criteria as well as the characterizations of uncertainty and expert judgment. Improving risk methodology is fundamentally an exercise in determining how these assumptions, all violated to varying degrees in the real world, can be relaxed.

The current MSRAM model assumes there is no explicit impact of an investment in deterrence.[5] The extension of the MSRAM methodology to join deterrence to the TVC paradigm will relax some of the assumptions underlying the current methodology. In so doing, the MSRAM model can more accurately portray the port risk environment, potentially resulting in improved investments in risk mitigation.

---

[5] The model does allow for its implicit consideration. This, however, can lead to inconsistency of results from port to port and scenario to scenario. It also makes it difficult to evaluate the deterrent effect of potential investments.

1.3. Overview of the Report

The remainder of this report is organized as follows. Chapter 2, "Performance Metrics," briefly describes the underlying motivation for performance measures in general, and the particular challenges of performance measures of security.

Chapters 3 - 5 focus on explicitly including deterrence in the MSRAM model. Chapter 3, "Deterrence," presents a discussion of deterrence based on deterring terrorism and is informed by traditional analysis of criminal behavior. This discussion brings to light assumptions violated by the MSRAM model: independence of events (because deterrence affects other parts of the model), linearity (through threshold effects) and perception bias (people are poor judges of probability).

Chapter 4, "Uncertainty and Possibility Theory," describes an alternative approach to gathering experts' subjective probabilities, used to quantify risk in the absence of data. This alternative approach is an application of possibility theory, which is a less restrictive framework than probability theory, requiring fewer assumptions. The possibility theory framework is more consistent with underlying uncertainties and thus, it will be argued, is better suited to the task of quantifying the impact of deterrence of a terrorist actor than the more traditional probability theory.

Chapter 5, "Application to MSRAM," applies this new tool set to the MSRAM model and uses it to extend the "detect-decide-engage" logic to incorporate deterrence, utilizing possibility methodology in a way compatible with the existing model. It also suggests a method for experts to collaborate in determining the impact of deterrence. This chapter addresses another facet of the independence assumption, focusing on spatial interactions within the port in relation to weapons of mass destruction (WMD) and area attacks.

Chapter 6, "Developing Robust Risk Estimates," takes up the limitations of the linearity of the MSRAM model chain, as currently implemented, and offers suggestions for extending the current model to more fully reflect real world complexities. The use of conceptual maps and influence diagrams are advanced in order to capture system effects and the non-linear nature of terror risk. Deterrence serves as an extended example in this section.

Finally, Chapter 7, "Recent Advances, Future Directions," describes advances in the analytics of spatial activity relating to port security that future versions of MSRAM might exploit. These advances include research into a similar problem, the spatial analysis of crime, as well as the general use of spatial methods and a particular GIS-based risk analysis tool from the Federal Emergency Management Agency (FEMA), called Hazards US (HAZUS).

Four appendices and a selected Bibliography complete the report.

2. PERFORMANCE METRICS

As the need to invest in security has increased, so has the need to develop improved measures of performance.[6] The establishment of risk-based frameworks has permitted the differentiation of ports according to types of risk. The process of managing the framework, establishing criteria for outside peer reviews, and other decisions such as the determination of evaluation criteria and method, is termed governance. Governance, while only touched on here, is a central part of successful implementation of the risk framework. For example, OMB encourages agencies to utilize outside review panels to augment internal working groups. Of course, each agency will establish governance procedures aligned with their overall strategic goals.

Key to making this process work is measurement. The model's basic elements: threat, vulnerability and consequence, are subject to continued refinement and elaboration. As the fundamental components of risk, these are the inputs to MSRAM. This report describes efforts to assess these components within the MSRAM tool, with particular emphasis on how to evaluate vulnerability. In addition, an effort is made to enable the USCG to standardize assessments across ports.[7] This involves bringing a particularly open and transparent approach in addition to experts' judgments.

2.1. Performance Measurement

Performance measurement is described by the GAO as, "the ongoing monitoring and reporting of program accomplishments, particularly progress towards pre-established goals."[8] Hence, it is more than developing metrics; it encompasses aligning programs with the organization's strategic goals, developing priorities, allocating resources in an effective manner and measuring outcomes. This is the case for tracking the effectiveness of both mitigation as well as research activities.

Characteristics of an effective performance measurement system include:

- Reliability, credibility
- Acceptance
- Timeliness
- Realism of goals
- Integration into agency decision-making

---

[6] See, Perl, Raphael, *Combating Terrorism: The Challenge of Measuring Effectiveness*, Congressional Research Service, The Library of Congress, November, 2005.

[7] See, US Government Accountability Office, *Risk Management: Further Refinements Needed to Assess Risk and Prioritize Protective Measures at Ports and Other Critical Infrastructure*, GAO-06-91, December 2005.

[8] See, US Government Accounting Office, *Performance Measurement and Evaluation, Definitions and Relationships*, GAO/GGD-98-26, April 1998.

Effective performance measures are now a key part of federal management practices, having been incorporated into OMB's review of submissions into the President's Budget, as implemented in OMB's Program Assessment Rating Tool (PART), a standard tool for agency evaluation.

The PART addresses:

- Program purpose and design
- Strategic planning
- Program management, and
- Program results.

PART questions address best practices in each of these areas. The PART requires an explanation and evidence for each answer. Evidence includes (but is not limited to) committee charters, Memoranda of Understanding (MOUs), documentation of processes or databases. Performance measures must measure outcomes, rather than activity.

2.2. Constructing Performance Measures

While in the past there has been emphasis on performance measures of process, outputs and outcomes, OMB has placed recent emphasis on measuring the efficiency of the process and the final results. Appendix A describes the OMB PART Process in more detail.

OMB guidelines for the development of performance metrics, especially for security-related "all-or-nothing" goals, include the development of proxy measures for cases where an event is catastrophic and so rare that it has not been observed.[9] The goal of preventing a major terrorist attack at a port is a case where the only acceptable level of success is absolute. Actual investments in security, in keeping with the concept of layered security, however, will address various sub-goals, which may have proxy measures for what cannot be observed. While a direct measure of port access might be the number of unauthorized intruders detected, proxy measures for port access may include related information on gates and guards, to be combined with crime statistics relating to unauthorized entry in the area of the port to support a broader view of port security.[10]

The next chapter discusses deterrence based on terrorism and on traditional analysis of criminal behavior, and describes how these affect the MSRAM model assumptions.

---

[9] See, Office of Management and Budget, *Performance Measurement Challenges and Strategies*, available at: http://www.whitehouse.gov/omb/part/challenges_strategies.html, June 18, 2003.

[10] Commercial products are available to permit tracking of crime trends and comparisons to regional and national levels. See, for example, CrimeCast's Cap Index (for Crimes Against Persons) census tract level products, at http://www.capindex.com/images/products/cutsheets/MapAnatomy.pdf .

3. DETERRENCE

As stated in the National Maritime Strategy,

> The basis for effective prevention measures – operations and security programs – is awareness and threat knowledge, along with credible deterrent and interdiction capabilities.[11]

Deterrence in the context of terrorism is not an easy subject, and has been gaining attention only recently. However, its take-up remains slow; it was not mentioned at all in a recent 450-page report on modeling threat anticipation.[12] Incorporating the role of deterrence in mitigating threats is examined here, with expert judgment as the principal input, due to the lack of historical sources of information. In other contexts, deterrence has been the subject of study for many years, primarily focused on the strategic theatre and nuclear exchange between superpowers, generally referred to as "classical deterrence." The concept of cumulative deterrence, in contrast, has been advanced to describe situations of continuing (non-nuclear) conflict, and casts off the all-or-nothing framework.[13] Thus, each success in an exchange is viewed as having a cumulative impact on the behavior of the adversary. The concept of cumulative deterrence is useful in the context of port risk when applied to each probe or attempted penetration of the port security system. These become data points, adding to understanding of the terrorist's determination, and are incorporated in subjective assessments of capability and success.

3.1. Risk Reduction

Risk reduction through security investments based upon deterrence is best analyzed in a manner that accounts for the relationship between the threats, consequences and vulnerabilities that comprise risk. The relationship between threat, vulnerability and consequence, in the context of terrorist risk, is often more complex than what can be represented by a multiplication of scores representing these factors. The intent of the terrorist gives rise to inter-relationships among threat, vulnerability and consequence.[14] MSRAM handles this by treating attacks and their consequences as separate events.[15]

---

[11] White House, 2005 National Maritime Strategy, Washington D.C., http://www.whitehouse.gov/homeland/maritime-security.html.

[12] See, Ackerman, Gary et al., *Literature Review of Existing Terrorist Behavior Modeling*, The Center for Nonproliferation Studies, Monterey Institute of International Studies, August, 2002.

[13] See, Almog, Doron, "Cumulative Deterrence and the War on Terrorism," *Parameters*, Winter 2004-05, pp. 4-19.

[14] See, for example, Darby, John (b), *Evaluating Terrorist Risk with Possibility Theory*, Los Alamos National Laboratory, LA-14179, November 2004.; and, Volpe National Transportation Systems Center (b), *Port Security Metrics: Performance Measure Model Options*, Final Draft, January 2006.among others.

[15] This method reduces the degree of error in final risk estimates if probabilities/possibilities are near 0.5. Other methods to account for the interactions between T, V, and C would be more accurate as probabilities/possibilities move away from 0.5. This is particularly relevant for security issues where rates of attack are often very close to zero.

3.2. Views of Risk

The literature on behavior under uncertainty addresses perceptions of risk and associated biases by individuals. For example, it is well known that individuals downplay common risks, while they exaggerate rare ones. Unusual risks are judged to be more likely than they actually are. Also, perceptions of personified risks exceed anonymous risks.[16] Lack of control also exaggerates the perceived risk of a given situation, helping to explain, for example, the fear of flying.[17] Perceptions can be managed in order to intensify the perceived risk of an act, which can in turn deter it.

The literature also indicates systematic differences between subjective, self-reported risk assessments (however biased) and actual behavior towards risk,[18] further complicating the issue.

3.3. Risk, Deterrence, and Ports

How can this information be used to understand deterrence at a port? After all,

> Some terrorist groups, however, commit terrorist acts without regard to their own personal risk. They will never be easily deterred. No amount of credible deterrent capability can guarantee that attacks by such groups will be prevented.[19]

The introduction of obvious operational risk to a terrorist's mission must be a key element in a security strategy, and should be measurable so as to track its effectiveness. A terrorist may not be deterred by the thought of being captured, imprisoned, or dying. Key, then, is deterrence via credible threat(s) to the mission by disruption and the addition of operational uncertainty and risk.[20]

3.4. Crime and Criminal Behavior

The literature on crime and criminal behavior informs our understanding of deterrence at the tactical level. Limited experience with controlled experiments indicates that criminal activity is subject to a strong displacement effect; a ubiquitous police presence in one area simply moves crime to less-policed areas. This could have strong implications for

---

[16] These behaviors are exploited by, for example, insurance agents, as they are careful to explain the particulars of coverage against some disaster in a policy to the potential buyer.
[17] By any reasonable measure, driving is many times more risky than flying, yet the sense of control helps alleviate the fear of being behind the wheel.
[18] See, Viscusi, Kip and William Evans, "Behavioral probabilities," *Journal of Risk & Uncertainty*, Vol 32, 2006, pp. 5-15.
[19] See, The National Strategy for Maritime Security, at http://www.whitehouse.gov/homeland/maritime-security.html .
[20] See, for example, Davis, Paul and Brian Michael Jenkins, *Deterrence & Influence in Counterterrorism: A Component in the War on al Qaeda*, RAND National Defense Research Institute, 2002.

port security.[21] It also highlights the need to examine these concepts spatially, which will be outlined later.

Deterrence may also be achieved by raising operational risk over a particular threshold. In a study of high-level drug dealers, the risk of interdiction had to reach 40 percent before considering an operation too risky.[22] Such thresholds may exist in the context of terrorism and threats to port security, and, if they do, they can be used to the advantage of the defender through strategies that maximize the perception of capture risk or, perhaps more significantly, mission failure and to prevent potentially wasteful investments above the threshold.

There has also been much study of deterrence with respect to the relationship between murder rates and the threat of capital punishment, as well as more recent studies of "right-to-carry" laws, which concern the relationship between violent crimes and laws allowing concealed weapons.[23] However, many of these studies utilize incomplete data. In the face of such problems, experts' opinions can be more accurate than statistical techniques designed for more data-rich situations.

3.5. Risk Biases

Individuals, in general, also have measurable biases as they perceive the lethal risks they face. This has been studied in the context of health and safety, and may only be loosely associated with risk taking behavior associated with port security. Still, biases towards overstating rare risks and the underestimating of common risks were found, as was an anchoring effect.[24] Anchoring is the effect of uninformative (perhaps even random) prior information on risk estimates.[25]

3.6. Risk Analysis and Deterrence

The measurement of deterrence required under the current implementation of MSRAM requires a subjective estimate of the effect of any particular investment aimed to thwart a given attack. The National Institute of Standards and Technology (NIST) has developed

---

[21] See, Di Tella, Rafael and Ernesto Schargrodsky, *Using a Terrorist Attack to Estimate the Effect of Police on Crime*, Draft working paper, Harvard University and Universidad Torcuado Di Tella, respectively, February 2002.

[22] See, Layne, Mary et al., "Appendix C: Prior Research," *Measuring the Deterrent Effect of Enforcement Operations on Drug Smuggling, 1991-1999*, Office of National Drug Control Policy, Available at www.whitehousedrugpolicy.gov/publications/enforce/measure_effect_2001, March 2002.

[23] See, for example, Goertzel, Ted, *Econometrics as Junk Science*, Rutgers University, monograph; expanded form of article published in *The Skeptical Inquirer*, Vol 26:1, January/February 2002, pp. 19-23.

[24] See, Armantier, Olivier, *Estimates of own Lethal Risks and Anchoring Effects*, manuscript, Department of Economics, University of Montreal, August 2005.

[25] A classic example is to take a survey of individuals on what they would estimate to be the population of Turkey. If before being asked, they are told it might be 10 million, or 50 million, or 100 million, these pseudo-facts influence the answers given.

software for risk analysis that includes the risk of terrorism.[26] Their methodology, based upon insurance industry techniques, is extended to terror risk through the use of expert judgment. They include use of Monte Carlo methods to quantify the range of possible outcomes, and in this way develop a measure of the risk. This methodology, while significantly different from MSRAM, keeps with general guidelines on risk analysis; both, however, compare overall risk by the determination of total risk shares.[27]

3.7. Handling the Problem of Risk

This chapter has described the first simplifying assumption the MSRAM model makes, namely independence of events, which is violated because deterrence incorporates learning behavior. In addition, since deterrence involves threshold effects, the assumption of linearity is also violated. The next chapter, Uncertainty and Possibility Theory, describes an appropriate tool set for addressing these issues by gathering the subjective probabilities from experts (necessary due to the absence of data), in a manner consistent with the underlying uncertainties inherent in the problem. This is an application of the theory of evidence termed possibility analysis, a less restrictive framework than probability theory and, therefore, better suited to defining risk amid uncertainty.

---

[26] See, for example, Chapman, Robert and Chi Leng, *Cost-Effective Responses to Terrorist Risks in Constructed Facilities*, National Institute of Standards and Technology, US Department of Commerce, NISTIR 7073, March, 2004.
[27] See, for example, Willis, Henry et al., *Estimating Terrorism Risk*, RAND Corporation, 2005.

4. UNCERTAINTY AND POSSIBILITY THEORY

Uncertainty may arise from ignorance, data variability, unknown ranges of values or directions of a model's input, or the outright lack of extant data. The latter is the (fortunate) truth for port security, since terrorist attacks at ports are rare enough that a suitable historical dataset does not exist. Overarching frameworks are currently being developed that permit examination of various forms of uncertainty and evaluation of their consequences.[28]

4.1. Problems with Probability

No degree of statistical expertise can bring truly meaningful results from analysis if the model's inputs are best guesses treated as certainty. In fact, such false precision can be potentially dangerous, leading decision-makers to gloss over alternate, nearly-as-likely scenarios.

> In order for the analysis ... to be scientifically credible, uncertainty must be accounted for properly. [Possibility theory] allows the analyst to express how much is known and how much is not known honestly.[29]

But isn't this why we use probability in the first place? Yes, except, as noted above, humans are highly fallible estimators of probabilities, subject to a variety of biases. It has been demonstrated that, "[S]ubjective estimates do not conform to the requirements of probability theory..."[30] Probability's faults can be seen, for example, in how easy it is to "trick" people into accepting the wrong answers to probability-based questions.[31] Therefore, in cases such as port security, where estimates must rest with people's judgments (even experts'), a framework that takes into account these uncertainties and mitigates bias would make the end results more accurate and thus, more useful.

---

[28] The software available at http://iridia.ulb.ac.be/pulcinella facilitates comparison among four kinds of uncertainty propagation, including possibility. From the website: "The key for Pulcinella's comparison power lies in the separation made between the process of modelling the structural knowledge of a problem, and that of modelling its qualitative knowledge. Once a structural model has been decided, we can superimpose any of the available uncertainty calculi on it. This comparison power can be useful for educational purposes; it can also serve at the first stages of a knowledge engineering task, where alternative theories of uncertainty can be tested on a bench-mark in order to choose the one that best fits the target problem."

[29] See, Kikuchi, Shinya and Partha Chakroborty, "Place of Possibility Theory in Transportation Analysis," *Transportation Research: Part B*, Vol 40, 2006, pp. 595-615.

[30] See, Raufaste, Eric, Rui da Silva Neves, and Claudette Marine, "Testing the Descriptive Validity of Possibility Theory in Human Judgments of Uncertainty," *Artificial Intelligence*," preprint, p. 2.

[31] Among other things, one can demonstrate that MBA students are "irrational" with respect to determining the outcomes of a variety of decision games carried out in a classroom setting. The extensive literature on the subject is termed Prospect Theory, so-named by the originators of the field, Daniel Kahneman and Amos Tversky.

4.2. Approaches to Uncertainty

A body of theoretical literature has been growing since the 1960's that is now making available a new set of tools designed specifically to handle situations characterized by a lack of knowledge or situations where there is conflicting information. It is not always the case that people act irrationally when they act in opposition to a probability model; rather, we can adapt the model to fit individual's perceptions of subjective probability. These less restrictive approaches are shown to match people's understanding of various decision problems more closely and yield outcomes that are natural and understandable to those involved.

Of the approaches to counter this problem, possibility theory is the least restrictive. Following the woodworker's admonition to use "the right tool for the right job," possibility theory, which is well suited to applications where only expert knowledge is available, has recently been applied to terrorism risk at nuclear power plants.[32]

MSRAM requires that users generate scenarios that are risk scored and apply expert judgment on various categories of risk. These categories (artificially) do not overlap and, hence, categories that may be related are not considered in the context of one other. It also implies complete agreement from experts as to the risks, likelihoods of threats, consequences and vulnerabilities in each scenario. This probably does not reflect the actual process involved in scoring the scenario, nor does it permit tracking of the uncertainties surrounding each scenario in order to improve understanding over time. This is exactly the "false precision" alluded to above.

The underpinnings of possibility analysis are described next, followed by their application to deterrence in MSRAM.

4.3. An Outline of the Theory of Evidence, Possibility Theory and Uncertainty

Possibility Theory might more accurately be called "Possibility and Necessity Theory." Rather than using a single probability measure interpreted as the "odds" of an event, possibility theory requires two concepts to fully describe the potential outcome. These are termed the "possibility" and the "necessity" of the event. Some find it easier to think of them as "plausibility" and "certainty," rather than "possibility" and "necessity," and the reader should feel free to substitute these terms throughout the discussion. Possibility indicates how feasible an event is (even if it never happens) and necessity indicates how certain the occurrence of an event is. Each is described on a 0 to 1 scale. A necessary event must be possible but a possible event need not be necessary. Thus, the possibility value must always be greater than or equal to the necessity value.

One feature of the theory is that the possibility of an event (Event A) and its converse (Event B or Event C or … Event Z)[33] need not sum to 1.0, as required by probability

---

[32] See Darby, John (b).
[33] For simplicity of the example, events A through Z encompass all possible events and are mutually exclusive.

theory. In fact, they will always sum to a value greater than or equal to 1.0 (similarly, the sum of the necessities will always be less than or equal to 1.0)

4.3.1. Possibility (Π) and Necessity (N)

Let $\Pi(A)$ denote the possibility of event A and let $N(A)$ denote the necessity of event A. Also let $\Pi(A^C)$ denote the possibility of event A not occurring (i.e. Events B through Z) and let $N(A^C)$ denote the necessity of event A not occurring.

Then, these relate to each other as:

$$N(A) = 1 - \Pi(A^C) \quad \text{and} \quad \Pi(A) = 1 - N(A^C)$$

In words, then, if it is possible to some degree that A^C occurs, it must be less than entirely necessary for A to occur. Additionally, if it is necessary to some degree that A^C occurs, then A must not be entirely possible.[34]

Note that if even if the necessity of A^C is zero:
- The possibility of A^C can still be anywhere from 0 to 1.
- The possibility of A is 1.

Thus, the possibility of A and A^C can add up to more than 1. This is the crux of the difference between possibility and probability, mathematically outlined below.

4.3.2. Differences and Similarities between Possibility and Probability

Compare the arithmetic constraints imposed by both theories:

Probability*	Possibility**
$P(A) + P(A^C) = 1$	$\Pi(A) + \Pi(A^C) \geq 1$
	$N(A) + N(A^C) \leq 1$
$P(A \cup B) = P(A) + P(B)$	$\Pi(A \cup B) = \max(\Pi(A), \Pi(B))$
$P(A \cap B) = P(A) * P(B)$	$N(A \cap B) = \min(N(A), N(B))$
* Assuming A and B are independent events. If they are not, the formulas change slightly but do not affect the comparisons discussed here.	
** These formulas hold true even if A and B are not mutually exclusive.	

The Possibility constraints are far less restrictive than the probability ones (most easily observed by the use of inequalities), allowing for uncertainty to play a greater role in evaluation.

---

[34] In fact, if A^C is any way necessary, then A must be not at all necessary. i.e. If $N(A^C)>0$, then $N(A) = 0$.

4.3.3. Expressing Uncertainty and Confidence

The following illustrate how uncertainty and confidence may be expressed in Possibility Theory:

Total certainty of A   is expressed as $\Pi(A) = 1$ and $N(A) = 1$ and

Total certainty of A^C is expressed as $\Pi(A) = 0$ and $N(A) = 0$, and

Total uncertainty of A   is expressed as $\Pi(A) = 1$ and $N(A) = 0$

An event that is entirely not necessary has no constraints on possibility:
If $N(A) = 0$ then $\Pi(A) \leq 1$

An event that has some degree of necessity must be entirely possible:
If $N(A) > 0$ then $\Pi(A) = 1$

For example, "A is highly possible" could be expressed as:[35]
$\Pi(A) = 0.8$ and $N(A) = 0$

"A is somewhat certain to happen" could be expressed as:[36]
$\Pi(A) = 1$ and $N(A) = 0.3$

A measure of confidence has recently been proposed, denoted C(A), where

$C(A) = \Pi(A) + N(A) - 1$

This measure ranges from total affirmation of A, expressed as 1.0, to ignorance, where the possibility of A is equivalent to the possibility of not A, expressed as 0, to total non-affirmation, expressed as –1.0.

The combination of possibility and necessity into a new measure of subjective possibility has been proposed as follows:

$\Psi(h) = \frac{1}{2}[\Pi(h) + N(h)]$

This is the strict average of the possibility and necessity measures,[37] combined to form a "subjective probability."[38] This is another connection between possibility theory and application in the probability theory-based MSRAM.

---

[35] Note that the value 0.8 is merely an example and may not be an accurate cognitive map of "highly possible."
[36] Note that the value 0.3 is merely an example and may not be an accurate cognitive map of "somewhat necessary."
[37] Proposed by Didier Dubois and described in Raufaste, et al.
[38] Experiments with experts, such as radiologists, confirm its applicability, as described in Raufaste, et al.

4.3.4. How to solve the problem of measurement where there is insufficient data.

The main motivation behind this additional complexity is that it better fits the problems that arise from uncertainty due to a lack of or incomplete knowledge

> (I)t is not clear that incomplete knowledge should be modeled by the same tool as variability. One may argue ... that the lack of knowledge is precisely reflected by the situation where the probability of events is ill-known, except maybe for a lower and an upper bound, or ... if only expert knowledge is available.[39]

Indeed, this is the very situation in which we find ourselves. But does it work? The theory has been refined and extended for decades, and applications are just now being published, but the results of experiments using panels of experts have been positive.[40]

4.3.5. Letting Go of Probability

There has been a great appreciation of the application of probability to our daily lives for some hundred years. The study of probabilities and risk[41] evolved in the context of games of chance and was advanced by the great French mathematicians of the seventeenth century.[42] The modern system of markets and insurance provided great benefits based on these precepts; however, they are not *always* the appropriate solution. To quote from Darby,

> In probability theory, the *degree of belief is the probability*; in possibility theory *the degree of belief is used to determine the possibility*.[43] [emphasis added]

and,

> Probability, as a normative framework, however, might not always be applicable to situations that humans face. Thus, there is no reason, in the general case, to believe that human judgments of uncertainty must be probabilities. As Shafer remarked, generally, the objective probabilities associated with possible events are not known, and "if we know the chances, then we will surely adopt them as our degrees of belief. But *if we do not know the chances, then it will be an extraordinary coincidence for our degrees of belief to be equal to them*."[44] [emphasis added]

In other words, when we invoke the word "risk" in the context of security, it is not always necessary or appropriate to quantify and manage the problem through use of strict probability. We need not inherit the (ill-suited) restrictions of probabilistic formalism, in the name of rigor. In fact, these restrictions can lead us to believe in the (false) precision

---

[39] See, Dubois, Didier, "Possibility Theory and Statistical Reasoning," *Computational Statistics & Data Analysis*, Elsevier Articles in Press, 2006.
[40] See, Raufaste, et al.
[41] Poisson invented the distribution that bears his name in order to study the fairness of judicial outcomes.
[42] See, Peter Bernstein, Against the Gods: The Remarkable Story of Risk, for a financial perspective.
[43] See, Darby, John (b), *Evaluating Terrorist Risk Using Possibility Theory*, Los Alamos National Laboratory, LA-UR-04-0904, undated, footnote on page 2.
[44] See, Raufaste, et al, pp. 1-2, quoting Shafer, in *A Mathematical Theory of Evidence*, Princeton University Press, 1976, p. 16.

of the results and influence decisions in ways that may actually *increase* risk. For example, a "precise" rank order of the top 10 threats may fail to include a substantial threat with a high degree of uncertainty (resulting in a low ranking). Despite the gravity of the threat, attention and investment may be diverted from it due to the falsely precise lower ranking. Again, the concept is "the right tool for the right job."

As was mentioned earlier, Darby has used possibility theory and developed software to calculate the risks of terrorist attack on nuclear power plants. He describes the move away from probability as follows:

> The restriction that probabilities sum to unity poses a problem: "The risk from a terrorist attack includes the likelihood that an attack occurs. The probability that an attack occurs is 1.0 minus the probability that an attack does not occur, but there is insufficient information to assign a probability to an attack not occurring: is it 0.5, 0.9, 0.99, 0.999...? [W]ith a probability measure we are forced to pay equal attention to estimating the likelihood that an attack does not occur (an event not of interest) as to estimating the probability than an attack does occur (an event of vital interest). The possibility that an attack occurs can be the same even if different possibilities are assigned to an attack not occurring; thus, using a possibility measure we can focus on the event of interest, an attack occurring, without focusing too much attention on an attack not occurring.[45]

Furthermore, since we are always faced with cases where there are insufficient data about the likelihood of extremely small probability events with large consequences, the biases to which people are prone only makes the situation more complex. Better to avoid the restrictive framework of probability altogether.

4.4. Sample Possibility, Necessity and Uncertainty Calculations for the Interdiction Chain

Uncertainty of intelligence is modeled in MSRAM as a triangular distribution, as in Figure 1.[46] This approach is the simplest way to account for a range of uncertainty while representing an upper and lower bound as well as a mid-point describing the most likely value. It is commonly employed for "rough modeling when actual data is absent."[47] The assumption embedded in this distributional form is that there in no chance, however small, that the parameter of interest takes on values outside the range (a, b). It would be possible to employ a similar triangular shape and account for the range of uncertainty in the estimates with the addition of the concepts of possibility and necessity, with uncertainty being calculated along the way, using the possibility measures.

---

[45] See, Darby, John (b).
[46] USCG briefing to DTRA and Volpe Center staff, January, 2006.
[47] See, Appendix E: Probability Distribution functions, in @RISK: Risk Analysis and Simulation Add-In for Microsoft Excel, Release 1.1 User's Guide, 1992.

Figure 1: Triangular Distribution of Estimates of Π(A)

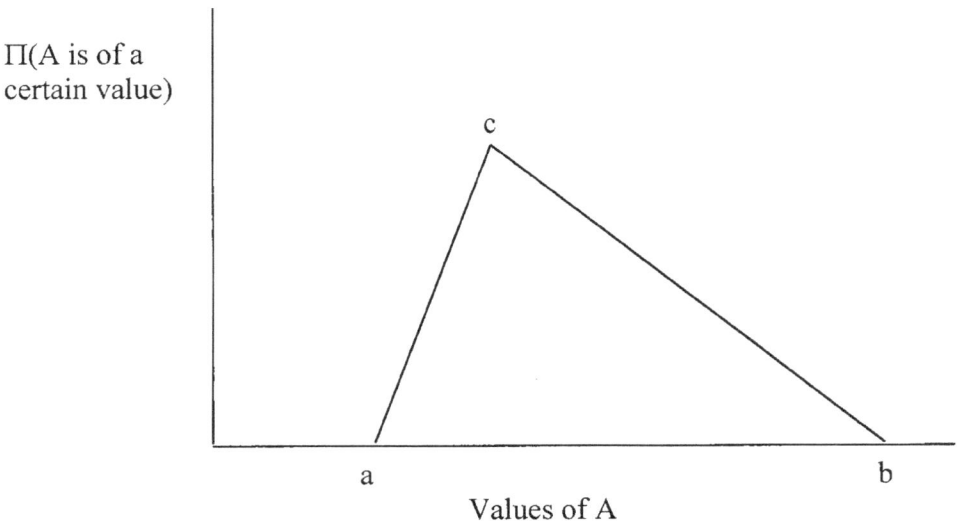

Let us first interpret the distribution above as the possibility that a specific security program has a deterrent effect modeled in this way. So, we think it could have as low an effect as possibility a, or as high as possibility b, but most likely the effect will be possibility c. This generally results from either a single subject matter expert's opinion or from a consensus estimate.

Let us focus on the Decide-Engage portion of the interdiction chain. The MSRAM methodology requires that a set of subjective probabilities be entered into the System Security Calculator. These come from a group estimate or subject matter expert. Consider now the case of determining the acceptable time for response to a particular attack mode, and the requirement that it be necessary that the response occur within a certain time.[48] This frames the question differently, and is in keeping with the understanding that while it is possible to arrive within some timeframe, it is also necessary to arrive within a certain time, depending upon the nature of the event.

---

[48] This strict boundary requirement may come from a set of operational orders, while the expert judgments are informed by the results of drills under various weather conditions, for example.

Figure 2: Sample possibility Distributions

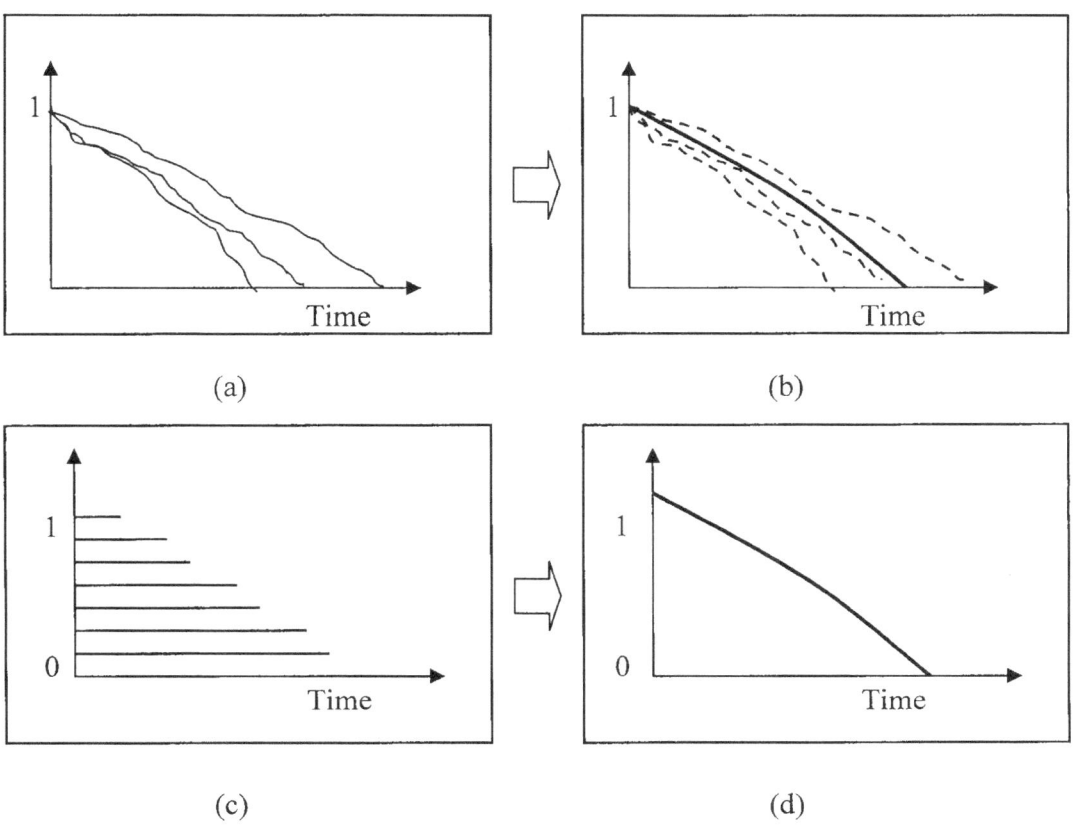

The graphs in Figure 2 demonstrate the creation of possibility distributions for such a delay.[49] For example, a group of subject matter experts is asked to determine the acceptable delay before engagement, essentially interpreted as the acceptable decision time. This has the effect of linking what are in fact dependent events, since the decision time is likely to depend upon the nature of the engagement.[50] In Figure 2(a), each line is the result of the opinion that the time is acceptable. Zero delay is always acceptable, and as delay time increases there is some decrease in acceptability until there is zero acceptance of delay (decision time). Different experts will likely have their own opinions as to the acceptability of a particular delay, so some method of deciding on a representative possibility needs to be determined, the results of which are shown in Figure 2(b). Another approach would be to represent each individual's measure of acceptable delay as a line extending from left to right, as in Figure 2(c). Ranking these in

---

[49] This discussion follows from Kikuchi and Chakroborty, 2006.
[50] The nature of the relationship between decision time and type of engagement is apt to be complex and non-linear. The detection of what is considered a minor event is likely to bring about a quick decision to act. The degree of uncertainty concerning the level of the event is also going to affect the decision time, so making this explicit will aid the understanding of the decision process.

order and finding the edge of this sample results in a possibility distribution, as in Figure 2(d).

There is uncertainty inherent in the arrival at the scene, given a certain departure time. Going back to the triangular distribution, the diagrams in Figure 3 demonstrate the effect of increasing the decision time on the likelihood of arriving in time to successfully engage.

Figure 3(a) shows that with a short decision time, a successful interdiction is possible, though not guaranteed (certain). Shifting the departure time, by increasing the decision time has the effect of decreasing the possibility of arriving in time for a successful engagement, and likewise increasing the possibility of an arrival too late, as seen in Figure 3(*b*).

Recall the proposed confidence measure, $C(A) = \Pi(A) - \Pi(A^C)$. This can be evaluated for particular shapes of the possibility distributions, as in the case here where A represents an acceptable arrival time, and A^C is a too late arrival.

Similarly, where $\Psi(h) = \frac{1}{2}[\Pi(h) + N(h)]$ is the measure of the subjective probability of arriving in time, this is a means by which to take the possibilistic measures and transform them into measures conformable to the MSRAM process. The next chapter describes the application of this approach to MSRAM through extension of the interdiction chain to include deterrence. Since the effects of various deterrence options can naturally be expressed as what is possible, rather than what is probable, given a lack of sufficient data, this framework is in general more suited to the nature of the problem.

Figure 3: Triangular Possibility Distribution of Arrival Time

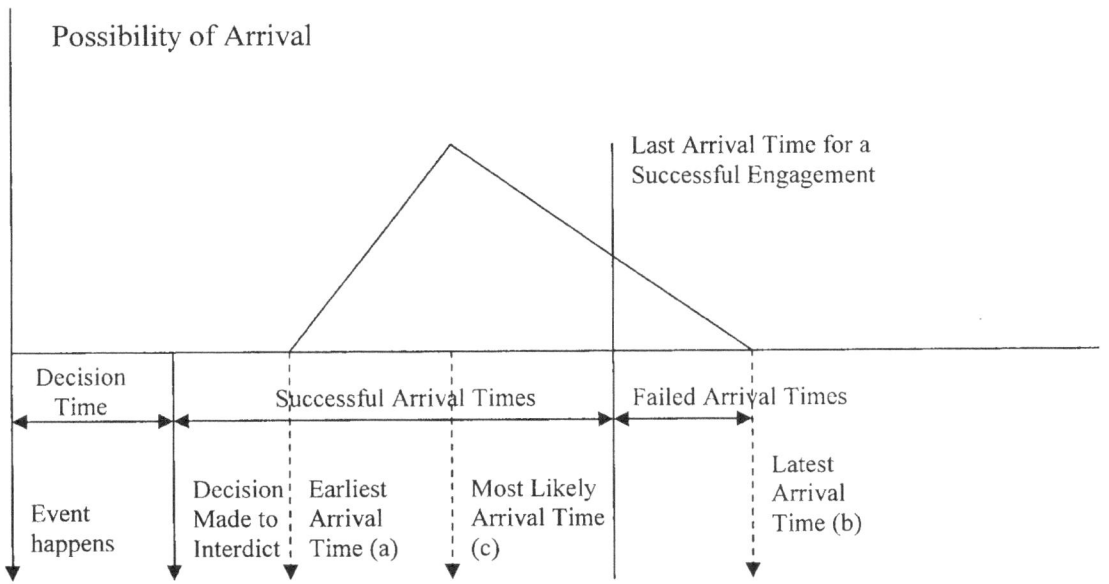

a) Short Decision Time and Possible Success

$\Pi(Success) = 1$; $N(Success) > 0$; $\Psi(Success) > 0.5$
$\Pi(Failure) > 0$; $N(Failure) = 0$; $\Psi(Failure) < .5$
$\Pi(Success) > \Pi(Failure)$; $\Pi(Success) + \Pi(Failure) \geq 1$
$C(Success) > 0$

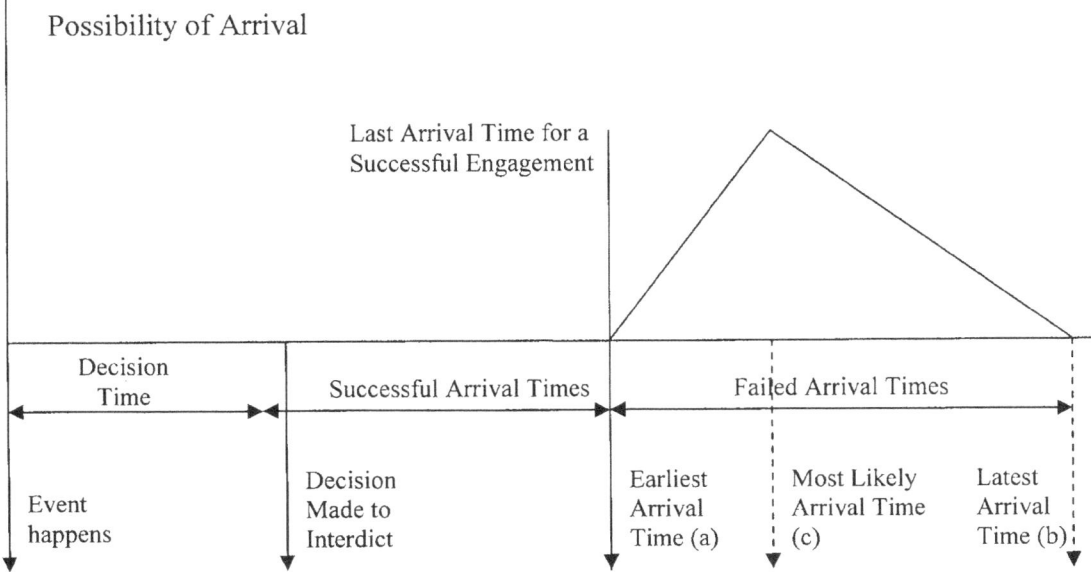

b) Long Decision Time and Impossible Success

$\Pi(Success) = 0$; $N(Success) = 0$; $\Psi(Success) = 0$
$\Pi(Failure) = N(Failure) = 1$; $\Psi(Failure) = 1$
$C(Success) = -1$

5. APPLICATION TO MSRAM

MSRAM is a software tool that calculates a risk index number (RIN) based on a well-known and standard risk methodology, described earlier as the Threat-Vulnerability-Consequence (TVC) paradigm.[51]

The system requires that targets be defined according to a set of attributes, including their availability and their associated maximum consequences. Threat values come from intelligence input.[52] Assessing a target's "Max Consequence" involves a series of factors:

- Death/Injury
- Primary Economic
- Secondary Economic
- Environmental
- National Security
- Symbolic

5.1. An Approach to Adding Deterrence to MSRAM through Vulnerability

Vulnerability, the descriptor of the (lack of) resistance of the target to attack, is determined in MSRAM by the "System Security Calculator."[53] This requires the user to enter into appropriate dialog boxes probability estimates for the likelihoods that the operators of the facility will successfully interdict the threat before the attack occurs. These interdiction likelihood estimates are based upon the following (assumed independent) events taking place:

> DETECT: Locate and identify entity as anomalous, or suspicious
>
> DECIDE: Identify as hostile and decide to engage (obtaining relevant permissions as needed)
>
> ENGAGE: Capability to stop the attack (including having enough time)

Each of these steps is associated with a subjective probability estimate, which, when multiplied together, calculate the probability of interdiction. It should be noted that the narrative accompanying the dialog boxes for these three items indicates that they are not

---

[51] This section is aimed at describing how to extend the "detect-decide-engage" chain to include deterrence. For details on the MSRAM application, see, "MSRAM Training and Software Manual," and its appendices, with Appendix 5 describing the MSRAM Scoring Methodology.

[52] As mentioned earlier, the uncertainty surrounding threats is modeled as a triangular probability distribution.

[53] The calculator is currently optional. A comprehensive inclusion of deterrence into MSRAM modeling would entail the calculator becoming a required step in the determination of Vulnerability.

really independent,[54] despite the formulas treating them as such. This creates a potential interpretation problem because the actual calculations do not faithfully reflect the intention of the user. Consideration should be given to revising this in a future version of MSRAM.

Adding "Deter" to the "Detect-Decide-Engage" chain of MSRAM calculations is straightforward if we employ the conversion from subjective possibility to subjective probability of deterrence, namely $\Psi(h) = \frac{1}{2}[\Pi(h)+N(h)]$. The chain, described in the MSRAM manual as a series of multiplicative probabilities, becomes:

$$\text{DETER} \times \text{DETECT} \times \text{DECIDE} \times \text{ENGAGE}$$

and consistency with the existing MSRAM application is retained. Thus, a connection is established between the probability methods in MSRAM and possibility metrics. An alterative approach would be to redo the underlying calculations following possibility theory.

Deterrence is a concept that has always been in the background of the analysis.[55] The intent here is to bring it out into the open in a manner that is clear and consistent with the subjective assessments already used by subject matter experts. In this regard the use of possibility metrics meets the stated objective.

5.2. An Alternative Link between Probability and Possibility in MSRAM

There have been frequent attempts at turning language-based ideas of likelihood into probabilities.[56] This literature, (for which an example is provided in Appendix C) aims to turn imprecise linguistic descriptions into more concrete and unambiguous estimates of probability, and offers even greater potential for application in possibility-based analysis. Possibility metrics express ambiguity and uncertainty and provide tools consistent with the problems faced by decision-makers rather than trying to fit probabilities into every situation, even when no data support them.

The imprecise language suggested in Appendix C may seem to make the model less precise, but actually increases its usability and accuracy by taking into account the uncertainty inherent in the experts' judgment.

Finally, it is easy to imagine Delphi-like groups building possibility distributions for deterrence and other aspects of risk. Appendix D describes the Delphi process in more detail.

---

[54] See, *MSRAM Training & Software Manual*, undated, on page 27, the example describes the user's entry into "Decide" as requiring an evaluation and incorporation of the passage of time into the probability value entered into the slot, which would, in turn, influence the ability to successfully "Engage" the threat.

[55] Personal communication, 16 January 2006, between Volpe Center staff, US Coast Guard and ABS Consulting, DTRA Headquarters, Fort Belvoir, VA.

[56] See, Beyth-Marom, Ruth, "How Probable is Probable? A Numerical Translation of Verbal Probability Expressions," *Journal of Forecasting*, Vol 1, 1982, pp. 257-269.

5.3. Recommendations for Improving the MSRAM Process

5.3.1. Deterrence

The GAO's recent report on the implementation of risk management methods noted that,

> The Coast Guard's tools for assessing risk currently do not take into account (1) reductions in vulnerability that stem from...actions such as security patrols or... monitoring or (2) the effect that multiple strategies (such as fencing and guards) may have on reducing vulnerabilities. As a result, the tools may overstate the degree of vulnerability that may exist.[57]

In response, the Coast Guard has taken steps to more rigorously assess vulnerability. One method of doing so is to explicitly include deterrence in the interdiction chain. The advantages of this inclusion can be compounded by the usage of linguistic descriptors (rather than "best-guess" numbers) in describing the impact of deterrence, and could easily be added into the MSRAM software. Furthermore, the creation of specific criteria on which to measure the efficacy of deterrence (and hopefully, in the future, other inputs) will help to make risk estimates comparable across ports.[58]

Consider an example of introducing an underwater barrier to prevent divers from entering a port's waters. Users would go back over each scenario in the MSRAM application (possibly using a Delphi process, for a suggested method, see the next section), indicating their assessment of the deterrent effect of the investment. The "System Security Calculator" dialog box could be updated to include Deterrence along with the already existing Detect, Decide and Engage.

Because the choice of one measure determines the value of the other, the user would choose whether they wanted to enter their degree of possibility or certainty (necessity). At that point, they will be presented with a slider bar to indicate the possibility or certainty using linguistic labels. Useful questions for a user to ask oneself are: "How plausible is this deterrent in this scenario." "If it is less than entirely plausible, how possible is it?" "If it is entirely possible, how certain am I that it will happen?" In this way, the user will know which slider to select, and the response will automatically determine the value for the other measure.

For example, if a user has determined that the deterrent effect of the barrier is highly probable in the given scenario, the system will automatically know it is not at all certain. It cannot be in any way certain to deter if it is not even entirely plausible. Similarly, if the user says the barrier is fairly certain to deter an attack, possibility will automatically be set to "entirely possible," as an event must be possible for one to have any degree of certainty it will happen.

---

[57] See, US Government Accountability Office, Risk Management: Further Refinements Needed to Assess Risk and Prioritize Protective Measures at Ports and Other Critical Infrastructure, GAO-06-91, December 2005.

[58] MSRAM Phase II will include checklists of defense capabilities allowing experts to have full information on available and installed deterrents in a standard way across ports.

The resulting entry of possibility or certainty would be converted to a subjective probability using the formula for Ψ discussed above. A sample of the dialog box is below in Figure 4. Should this method of entry gain acceptance, in the future, the entire dialog box could be converted and a more complete use of possibility theory can be implemented.

In this example, the experts would enter how possible (or certain) a deterrent the fence would be in stopping each attack scenario (divers used to plant a bomb, hijackers board a cruise ship, attack via small aircraft, etc.). After all scenarios have been considered, new risk scores would be calculated to determine the risk reduced by the fence. This could then be compared to other potential deterrent investments.[59]

Figure 4: Sample System Security Calculator Dialog Box

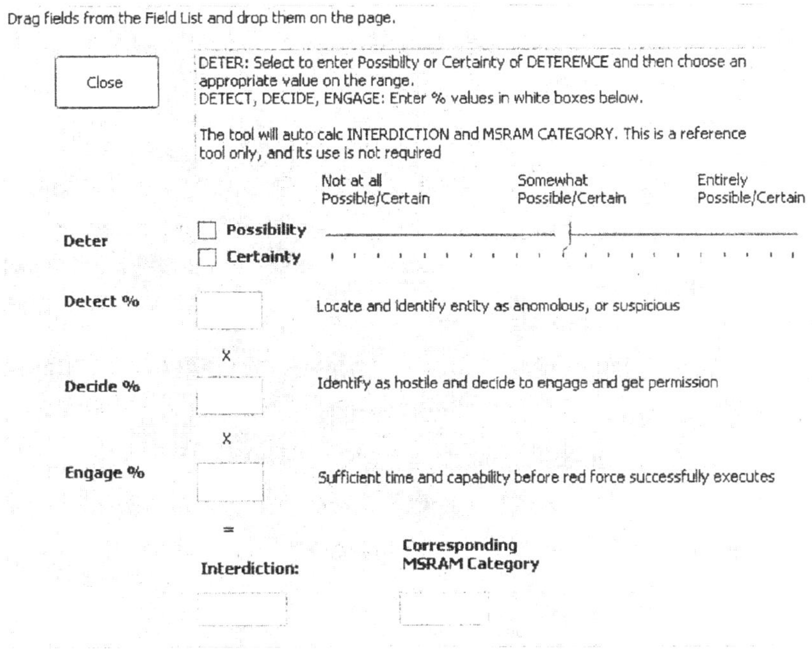

5.3.2. An Iterative Process to Determine Possibility Using Experts' Judgment

This section presents a suggested method for determining the possibility (necessity) of deterrence for a given scenario or investment. It is an application of the Delphi Method, a consensus-building process that allows for feedback among participants and mitigates

---

[59] The "change case" functionality being added with the Phase II release of MSRAM will make comparison across multiple runs easier.

the effects of a dominant personality. (For an overview of the Delphi Method, see Appendix D.)

First, a group of decision makers is convened.[60] The makeup of the group should encompass a broad range of skills and backgrounds and will likely be similar to the groups that make decisions on the likelihood inputs used in other parts of the interdiction chain (detect, decide, and engage).

The facilitator will present to the group the details of the scenario and/or potential deterrent, allowing anyone to ask questions. Once everyone has a sufficient grasp of the situation, all group members will be asked to individually and anonymously rate the possibility or certainty that the attack will be deterred. Participants will be able to justify their choice in two or three sentences. In cases where participants have entered extreme values (possibilities under 0.15 or necessities over 0.80, for example), they will be strongly encouraged to justify their response.[61]

After all responses have been collected, the facilitator distributes a summary of the results. Depending on the group size, this may be a list of all responses, a frequency distribution of responses, or other descriptive statistics. The summary should also include the justifications for particular values, with particular importance on the reasons for answers far from the average. Participants will have the opportunity to read over the results and send back comments. These comments can be general or specific responses (positive or negative) to the justifications of others' answers. As all answers and comments are anonymous, comments need not be related to the participant's original answer. In fact, if a particular justification has swayed his or her opinion, a response noting why this is the case would be highly encouraged.

After sufficient time, the facilitator collects the responses and distributes them to the group, again anonymously. At this point, participants will have the opportunity to enter a new response for the possibility/necessity of deterrence. For a second time, all participants are able to offer supporting comments, with special encouragement to do so for those with views outside the norm. The comments are distributed and the process repeats until a consensus is reached. Ideally, it should take two or three cycles for the consensus to emerge, though it is prudent to continue the process as long as opinions continue to shift from cycle to cycle.

Unresolved significant differences of opinion among the experts may result in the need to develop a tie-breaking strategy, such as a vote. Alternatively, each case may be treated separately or the worst case may be chosen, in keeping with the current MSRAM procedure.

---

[60] It is expected that early implementations of this process could involve the group meeting in one physical location working with pencil and paper. Later, this process could be moved to computers over a network so that the group need not be in the same room. The basic description of the process will assume the early version and the section will conclude with some comments about refinements that can be added with a computer-based process.

[61] Justification is not required, in order to prevent participants from entering values just above or below thresholds to avoid having to write a justification.

The method just described can be partially automated, with software presenting each participant with a slider similar to that seen in Figure 4, above. While all participants would still be able to enter justifications for their answers, the software could require justifications from those whose answers are significantly different from the average respondent (criteria could include one standard deviation or two levels of confidence, depending on the size of the group and the dispersion of responses). The combination and redistribution of the answers would be faster when done by computer and would likely increase the anonymity of the process. Furthermore, a voting process in the event of a stalemate can be faster, and (perhaps) more complex voting methods could be considered.

Transfer of the process to personal computers would also allow for the meeting to take place over multiple locations (i.e., each person in his or her own office or in different cities) and over a greater period of time (i.e. participants could log into the system at their convenience to enter votes and responses). This would be particularly useful if the Delphi method is adopted for other inputs in the MSRAM model.

5.3.3. Area Attacks

The current MSRAM model only incidentally includes area attacks and the use of WMD. Such scenarios are optional at the port level and only considered when the target is "Other – High Density Population Area." The ability to consider multiple types of WMD attacks and on specific parts of the port may enable better risk management. Similarly, area attacks that do not affect the populated area around the port, but may disable multiple sections of the port, also warrant similar treatment, likely with the use of spatial analysis techniques (these are mentioned in Section 6.4).

The Phase II implementation of MSRAM, not yet fielded, modified the calculation method for the determination of consequences, based upon user's suggestions. The MSRAM developers suggest that this will have an impact on the outcome of WMD scenarios.[62] The key concern among users was the size of the incremental jumps between levels on the consequence scale. This, as well as the use of mid-points in the range to perform the calculations of risk, has been adjusted in the new version. The user now has control over the consequence value, so that they can use their best estimate. These improvements to the model permit WMD scenarios to better represent the consequences of such attacks, and thereby more accurately reflect the subsequent risk calculated in the model.

---

[62] The magnitude of the differences would be compared by, for example, running similar scenarios through the two versions of the software and then making the comparisons as to the outcomes of consequence and risk.

5.3.4. A Systems Approach

In a larger scale, the determination of vulnerability reduction needs to be tracked through the system to account for the sum of its impacts. That is, a systems approach is required, since the nature of the problem is that there are likely to be tipping points, non-linearities, and the potential for complex interactions among system components that need to be accounted for. While complex, the benefits of such a method would make it possible to discover that enough investment has been made in an area, perhaps crossing a threshold beyond which another program would have no effect, be wasteful, or worse, be counter-productive. Chapter 6 discusses this concept in more detail.

The use of the cognitive maps (or influence diagrams) is suggested in the next chapter as a means of capturing the port-specific interactions among programs that, given the particulars of geography, layout, facilities, cargos, proximity to population, etc., make each port unique. These can be used to capture and transfer this knowledge and continually refine the understanding of how the parts interact. This is a systems approach, which will address the restrictions inherent in the linear approach of traditional TVC-based analysis.

6. DEVELOPING ROBUST RISK ESTIMATES

Possibility metrics provide a means of addressing the inherent "brittleness" of results derived from traditional probabilistic methods. With traditional probabilistic methods, if a subject matter expert is forced to choose a particular category of consequence, then that choice necessarily excludes all others. That is not true in possibilistic methods since the choices, in a real sense, overlap. Formally, there is shared membership in the set of choices. Thus, a fence designed to meet a security standard (in materials, height, knuckling, selvage, etc.) has membership in the group of security fences, but may also have partial membership in the group of crowd safety or ornamental fences (i.e. membership in each group need not be exclusive).

In the same way, the deterrence measure has a range and a membership in multiple categories. This can be interpreted as a robust estimation method. Robust estimation simply means that the model results can withstand partially faulty assumptions (i.e., "What if the underlying model is wrong?"). Rather than have the world turn out radically different than predicted by your model due to a single flawed assumption, a more robust method considers a range of options, assumptions, and even models, so that, in case you picked the wrong one(s) (i.e., the world is not as you hypothesized), you still have answers that are close to reality.

Continuing the fence example, a model designed to include the deterrent effect of fencing may not take into account situational factors that will affect its value. For example, should a port stack containers near a fence or allow vegetation to grow too close, the risk of a climb-over increases. Conversely, a fence paired with cleared zones and security lighting will provide a greater deterrent than a fence alone. A robust model is better able to handle these variations in application without explicitly including each situational factor in the model. This is particularly useful in cases where the extra factors are unknown, unexpected or unquantifiable. Possibility theory, through its explicit acknowledgment of uncertainty, is more robust than probability theory, which can attach a false precision to estimates of risk.

Robust methods have been shown to give better (cheaper, more efficient) answers in cases where there in uncertainty. More technically, a robust regression method might be chosen, for example, when the data have an outlier that would gain too much influence over the parameter estimates using a conventional (usually least squares) error structure. The estimator chosen is designed, in fact, not to fit the pattern of the data, but rather the pattern of the error structure, a subtlety often overlooked but very much to the point here. It is the pattern of errors, or, in the security context, adverse consequences, that drives the choice of model, whether in the context of regression modeling or in a risk management system aimed at minimizing the consequences of an adverse action.

6.1. Conceptual Maps

Conceptual maps provide a means of exploring the inter-relationships among a system's components, whether they are direct or indirect, positive or negative. Suppose, for example, an asset of high consequence was deemed vulnerable and as a result received a sufficient investment in security-related enhancements that, while less vulnerable, its perception as a symbolic target also increased significantly. This, in turn, could lead to an increased possibility of an attack. Enhancing an asset's value as a terrorist target in this way could undermine the benefit of the security investment, and perhaps lead to an overall increase in risk. The development of conceptual maps, explicitly linking this interaction between effects, could help prevent such a situation from actually occurring.

6.2. Ports as Complex Interacting Systems

Ports pose a wide variety of security challenges, since their mission involves the facilitation of the movement of goods representing the majority of the world's commercial activity. As has been noted elsewhere,

> Ninety-five percent of the world's goods – worth some $500 billion – move via marine transportation yearly to several hundred U.S. ports, in about five million containers.[63]

This key role in the supply chain makes them high value targets for terrorist attack. Recently, the port closure policy of the United States was clarified in The National Strategy for Maritime Security, which states that ports will not be shut down "as an automatic response to a maritime incident, as happened in the aftermath of the September 11, 2001 attack on the World Trade Center."[64] This has significance since it negates the commonly assumed default strategy of dropping anchor as a response to almost any port-related emergency, from loss of navigational aids to a disruption of cargo handling facilities. Continuity of operations is now emphasized.

The recent release of The National Strategy for Maritime Security identifies five critical strategic actions:

- Enhance International Cooperation
- Maximize Domain Awareness
- Embed Security into Commercial Practices
- Deploy Layered Security
- Assure Continuity of the Marine Transportation System

The need for flexibility of response is balanced against the requirement that there be standardized governance, and is motivated by the following:

---

[63] See, Walsh, David, "Maritime Security - Vulnerabilities acknowledged," *Homeland Defense Journal*, December 2004, p. 29.

[64] See, The National Strategy for Maritime Security, at http://www.whitehouse.gov/homeland/maritime-security.html and the eight implementation plans by the Department of Homeland Security at http://www.dhs.gov/dhspublic/interapp/editorial/editorial_0608.xml .

> Compared to commercial airports, seaports are generally more diverse in terms of their physical infrastructure and operations. As a result of this diversity in characteristics, each ship and port facility presents different risks and vulnerabilities. Port authorities are also very concerned with finding the right balance between standard and port specific security regulations. Ports seek a level of uniformity in security requirements because they are concerned that their customers will move their business to competing ports where their goods may be cleared more quickly. At the same time, ports do not want to be held to inflexible federal standards. They are concerned that setting security benchmarks may waste time and resources if those benchmarks are not applicable at their port given their particular commodity mix or other unique circumstances.[65]

These complexities lead to interactions among the parts that can be handled through application of port-specific conceptual maps, or influence diagrams.

Also, conceptual maps provide a record of the decisions taken by the panel of experts. In that way, they function as part of a knowledge management system. This is part of a systems approach to the problem of sorting out and quantifying the various, sometimes contradictory influences among the parts of a system, and may be of use in providing consistent use of MSRAM across ports.

6.3. Observable versus Unobservable Protection

As described in the NIST report, making one target harder introduces the possibility of a substitution effect, whereby a softer target is chosen, or complementary effects are produced, wherein,

> Under certain conditions, unobservable protective measures could reduce the probability of an attempt, both on the protected building and on nearby buildings as well.[66]

As described by insurers, "the conditional probability that one specific landmark is attacked will depend partly on its relative vulnerability, and partly on its intrinsic attractiveness as a political totem... [S]ome idea of event likelihood is needed for intelligent benefit-cost analysis."[67] The derivation of these subjective probabilities is therefore critical to understanding the real risk. In the absence of historical data this becomes particularly difficult. One suggestion for dealing with this issue is the creation of conceptual maps, described next.

6.4. The Use of Conceptual Maps

Conceptual maps can be used to determine the likelihoods required by an insurance-based methodology, as the following figures illustrate. Figure 5, below, reproduces part of a conceptual map of deterrence, aimed at the level of a national strategy. It includes the

---

[65] Taken from Frittelli, John, *Port and Maritime Security: Background and Issues for Congress*, Congressional Research Service, The Library of Congress, May 27, 2005.

[66] See, Appendix E: Substitution Implications of Risk Mitigation Activities, in Chapman and Ling, Cost-effective Responses to Terrorist Risks in Constructed Facilities, NIST, p. 119.

[67] See, Woo, Gordon, "Benefit-Cost Analyses for Malevolent Human Actions," Note prepared for the *Columbia/Penn Roundtable*, April, 2002.

addition of operational risk among the other factors that a national strategy might be able to influence. One conclusion that comes from this model is that, in the case of nuclear non-proliferation, an effective deterrent strategy is to announce, with a high degree of credibility, that the source of nuclear materials would be treated to same level of retaliation as the immediate user. Much of the utility of the approach derives from the ability to make the models more complex, while dealing at a level of abstraction such that the complexity does not overwhelm. A simple example using choice of driving speed will be used as an illustration of the way in which realism is added to a conceptual model. An example from the security domain is then presented.

Figure 6 provides a familiar context, a simple model describing the choice of highway driving speed. It is only a first pass at the influences on speed choice, and it lacks a key element in the decision-making process. The next diagram, Figure 7, demonstrates the additional complexity brought on by reconsideration of additional influences among the components of the model. Also, notice that the concept of a schedule has been introduced. In the prior model, only negative influences on speed choice were available. This new influence will help explain the tendency to choose a faster speed. Software is available to solve these types of models and to determine their tendency to reach equilibrium.[68]

The next figure, Figure 8, describes a notional diagram of a cognitive map describing security investment choices and their impact on the detect-decide-engage decision. Assembled by a single subject matter expert or a panel (perhaps using Delphi techniques), the goal would be to develop a richer understanding of the interacting influences on port security, including deterrence, by examining the influences of all the significant components at work. The first figure shows only the positive effects of investment in detection (say, through added patrols or closed circuit television) and engagement (say, through added forces and equipment to reach all points quickly and well armed). These investments will improve the capability to deliver a successful engagement. Figure 9, meanwhile, adds the impact of deterrence as well as the additional influence of investment in decision capability. The deterrence investment is positively related to the ability to successfully detect a threat, since there will be fewer alerts.

With the added focus on investment and the impact on timely decision making, the logic behind the investment (the business case) becomes clearer and is easier to articulate. The structure permits an evaluation of the portfolio of possible investments in each element in a consistent fashion, and the indirect impact of an investment can be made clear.

Finally, this analysis could be expanded to include a broader risk assessment and examine the effects of tipping an asset into a new risk category, for example.

Such maps will help illuminate the interactions between components, including feedback and feed-forward mechanisms, and provide additional information to experts making judgments about vulnerabilities. With further refinement of the mapping process, MSRAM formulas could incorporate this information through the use, in particular, of spatial analysis (discussed in Section 7.1).

---

[68] See more on cognitive maps in decision making at "More on fuzzy cognitive maps," www.edn.com/archives/1996/042596/09column.htm#fig2 and for software at www.syncopationsoftware.com/dpl.html , which describes the DPL tool.

Figure 5: Conceptual Map of Deterrence Strategy[69]

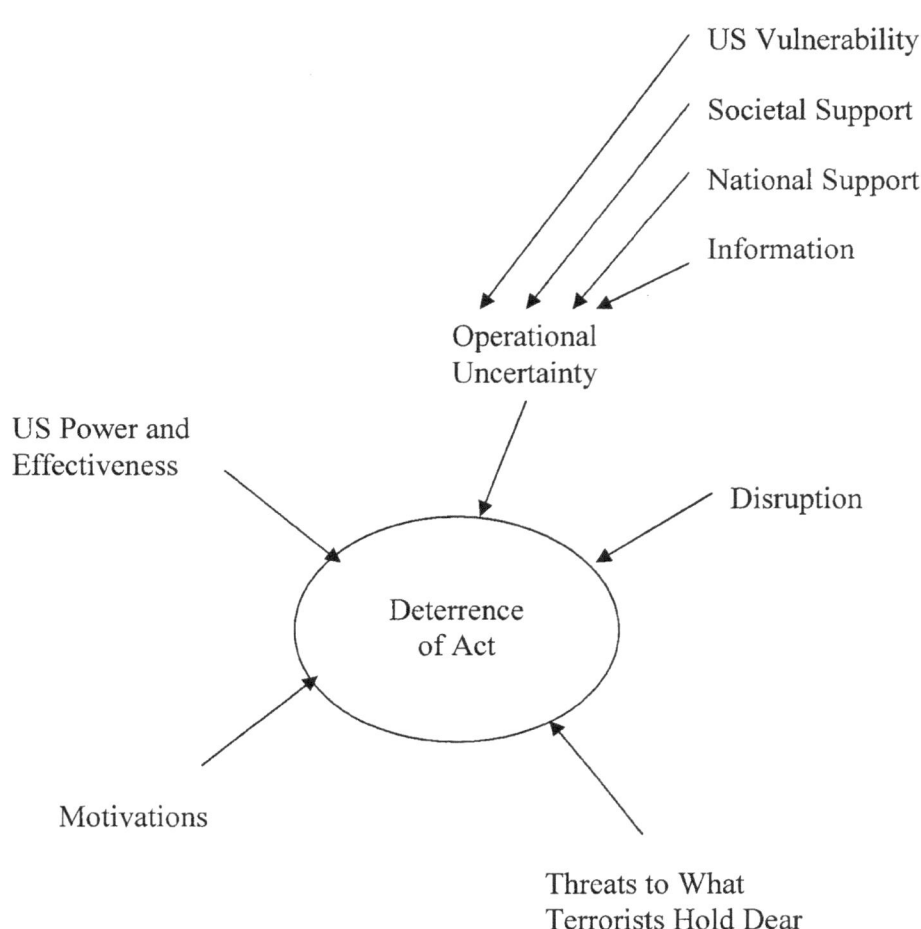

---
[69] Referred to as Cognitive Modeling in Davis and Jenkins.

Figure 6: Simple Example of Driving Speed Determination

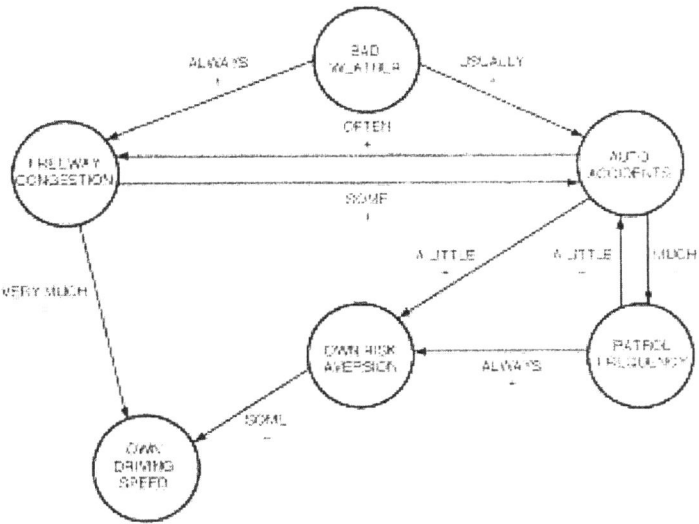

Figure 7: More Complex Driving Speed Decision Model

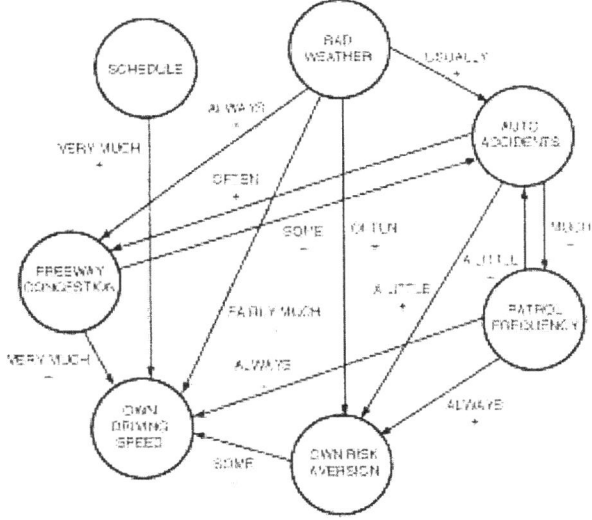

Figure 8: A Notional Example of the Influence of Deterrence on the Interdiction Chain

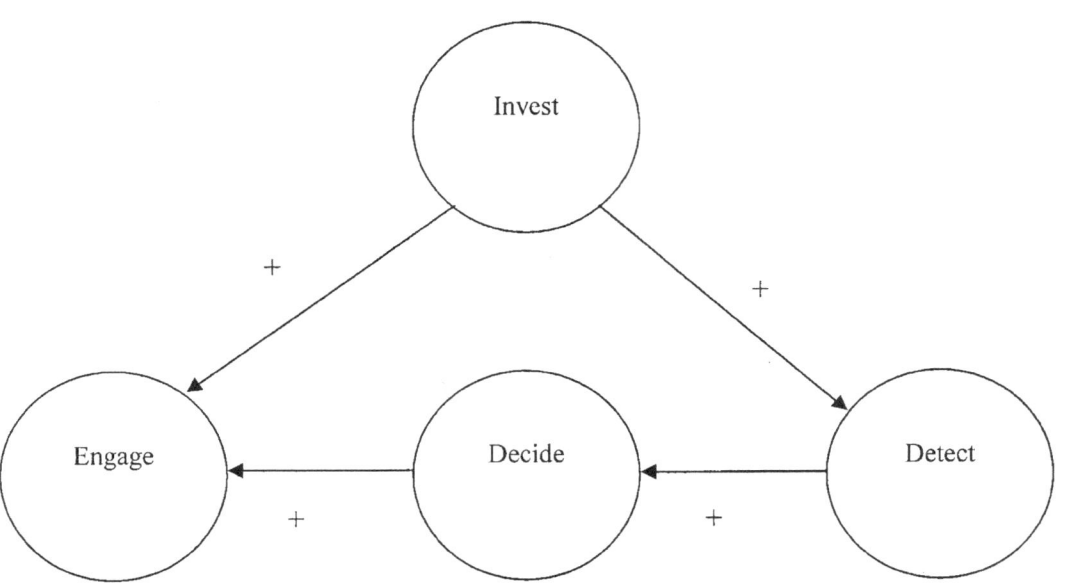

Figure 9: A Notional Example of the Influence of Investment on the Interdiction Chain, adding Deterrence and Interactions

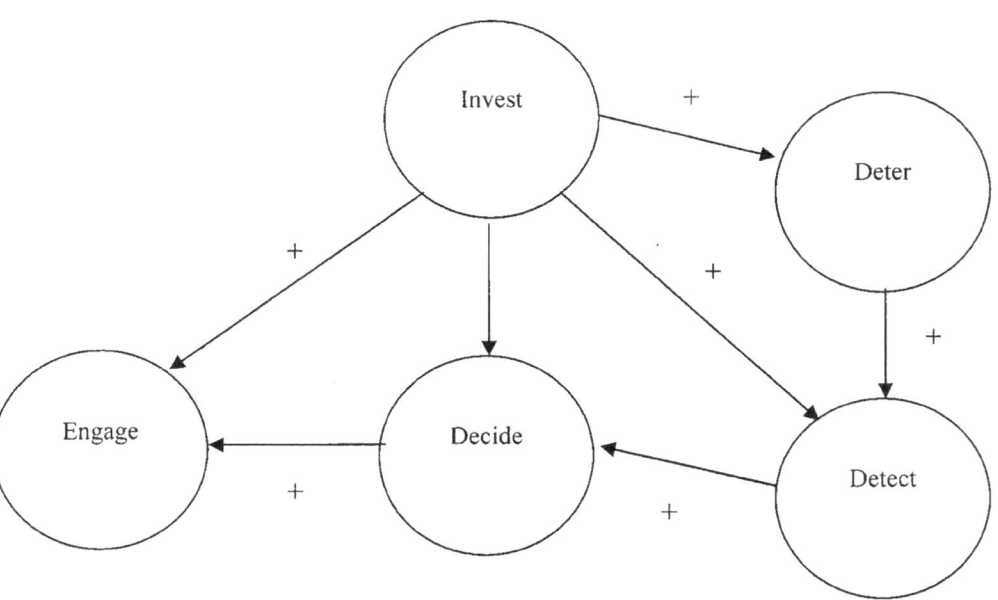

7. RECENT ADVANCES, FUTURE DIRECTIONS

It may seem premature to talk of future directions when the task of incorporating recent advances in decision theory into practice is so large. Many other areas of understanding that are expected to be of use in the security domain, however, are also advancing. This chapter looks at some of the recent advances that are of apparent relevance to security and potentially MSRAM. It then addresses specific recommendations for future work that might be undertaken to improve and enhance MSRAM and further relax the key assumptions of the model.

7.1. Recent Advances

Among the recent advances made that could have an important impact on security, those in the area of spatial analysis have particular relevance.

For instance, in addition to the improved use of expert knowledge amid uncertainty, ongoing work in the spatial analysis of crime deserves attention as well. The spatial dimension of port security has been largely ignored thus far, except to mention displacement effects. A recent analysis focuses on the geographic preferences of criminals and shows that these can be used to improve on current methods of mapping crime "hot spots."[70] The environment described is data rich, and permits the use of discrete choice modeling of criminal preferences. The prediction of criminal patterns in space can be useful in describing the overall security posture of an area. The presence of graffiti on a rail tank car is a sure sign that someone has breached the physical security of the facility. Hence, an improved understanding of the pattern of criminal behavior can be useful to the full characterization of the security of a port or other infrastructure. Since there is speculation that the knowledge and techniques of criminal enterprises are being transferred to terrorist groups, it is reasonable to suggest that information gained from analyses from the data rich (crime) and data poor (terrorism) environments could be fused to improve the understanding of both. Such data could be used as proxy variables in pursuit of performance measures in the absence of data.

Spatial techniques in econometrics have also been used to overcome the special issues presented by geographic data, and this offers a rich source of tools with which to address these problems.[71] Spatial tools include various other risk models.

A risk-based GIS platform in use by the Federal Emergency Management Agency (FEMA) is HAZUS-MH.[72] It consists of a full GIS system and underlying data sufficient to map risks of various natural hazards. The mapping interface would provide a useful

---

[70] See, Xue, Yifei and Donald Brown, "Spatial Analysis with Preference Specification of Latent Decision Makers for Criminal Event Prediction," *Decision Support Systems*, Vol 41, 2006, pp. 560-573.
[71] See, http://rri.wvu.edu/WebBook/LeSage/spatial/spatial.html, an online Spatial Econometrics textbook, which describes the techniques required when handling spatial data.
[72] The MH stands for multi-hazard.

means of displaying the risk data generated in MSRAM, perhaps adding the insights of location-based analysis.

RAMPART, developed by Sandia National Laboratories for use by the General Services Administration (GSA) after the Oklahoma City bombing, employs data from crime statistics and natural hazards data, as well, but also relies on expert knowledge input by users for terror risk assessment.[73]

7.2. Recommendations with Respect to MSRAM

Recommendations for improving MSRAM include (1) developing a conceptual map of MSRAM's logic flows, (2) incorporating the modeling of adaptive behavior into MSRAM, and (3) combining GIS and the Analytic Hierarchy Process with MSRAM.

A first step for any improvement for MSRAM would be to develop a conceptual map of MSRAM's overarching logic flows. As new learning develops, this map would enable MSRAM to be updated in a consistent manner. The maps can be expected to get quite complicated, allowing checks for consistency with other policy guidance as well as existing or new programs, easing the incorporation of new sub-systems. Thus, maps could be used to describe port components, their interactions and the interactions of the port itself to the larger threat environment.

The risk calculation in MSRAM is based on the assumption that the arrivals of ships into port result in either an attack or not, a binomial probability distribution. It assumes the likelihood of any event is independent of the other, and hence, follows a Bernoulli process.[74] This is likely not to be the case, since it is well known that adversaries learn and adapt to new circumstances. Researchers at MIT simulated a situation in which airport security was probed to determine if the security screening procedures would identify the terrorist, who would be picked out for additional scrutiny or pass through undetected. This simple adaptive behavior altered the effectiveness of the screening methods.[75]

Another possible improvement would be to combine GIS and the Analytic Hierarchy Process (AHP), as was done in risk analysis of hazardous materials shipments, a similar problem involving the incorporation of expert judgment. AHP was used to determine weights for a risk analysis; possibility methods can be used to determine the likelihoods of attack based on expert judgments, as well.[76] (See Appendix B for a discussion of AHP.)

---

[73] See, Chapman, Robert and Chi Leng, *Cost-Effective Responses to Terrorist Risks in Constructed Facilities*, National Institute of Standards and Technology, US Department of Commerce, NISTIR 7073, March, 2004.
[74] See, *MSRAM Training & Software Manual,* "Appendix 5, MSRAM Scoring Methodology."
[75] The so-called Carnival Booth algorithm, which simulated the effects of a randomized security regime.
[76] See, Huang, Bo, Cheu Ruey Long and Yong Seng Liew, "GIS-AHP Model for HAZMAT Routing with Security Considerations," *IEEE 6th International Conference on Intelligent Transporttaion Systems*, October, 2003.

MSRAM Phase II begins the process of looking at risk from a geo-spatial perspective by creating maps of risk around the port. Econometric spatial techniques, when applied, would allow analysis (reflected on the maps) to reflect the relationships that take into account the geometry, geography, and effects of one part of the port on another.

7.3. Adding Tipping Points and Non-Linearities to MSRAM

If terrorists have thresholds of deterrence and can be kept at bay once these have been achieved, it would be an unwise investment to keep increasing the level of security beyond the necessary point. Indeed, it may have the opposite of the intended effect, increasing the symbolic value of the target, as discussed above.

Tipping points and non-linearities are issues that affect the broad practice of risk management as applied to security and terrorism. Sponsoring a conference session at a meeting of the Military Application Society (MAS) of the Institute for Operations Research and Management Sciences (INFORMS) or similar organization, focusing on these issues would be useful to further understanding and implementing these concepts.[77]

---

[77] Another candidate would be the Society for Risk Analysis (SRA), which has its annual meeting each December. www.sra.org

APPENDIX A: OFFICE OF MANAGEMENT AND BUDGET'S (OMB'S) PERFORMANCE ASSESSMENT RATING TOOL (PART) PROCESS

OMB's approach to program management can be summarized as follows: (1) set stretch goals, (2) measure performance, and (3) optimize the portfolio of activities with a transparent decision process, including audits and internal and external review. Details on the process can be found at http://www.whitehouse.gov/omb/part/index.html.

The process emphasizes good governance and is a straightforward "carrot-and-stick" approach to getting a budget for a program. Agencies that perform well in their PART may receive more funding than they had requested, while those that do not demonstrate that they are efficient and effective could suffer budget cuts.

A sample of 64 Federal agency performance measures is can be found at an OMB website, www.whitehouse.gov/omb/part/performance_measure_database.xls . The range of agencies reporting is wide, but the majority of measures listed are either related to outcome (48 measures) or efficiency (15 measures). A lone output measure, land cleared and returned to productive use, was reported by the State Department.

In particular, performance measurement is described in examples in OMB's Frequently Asked Questions as excerpted below:[78]

What are outcomes and outputs?

An outcome refers to the events or conditions of direct importance to the public/beneficiary that are external to the program. An outcome answers the question "What is the program's goal or purpose?" For example, the goal of a job training program is to give someone the skills to find a job, as opposed to giving out a grant. An outcome measure may be the number and percent of people employed within six months of completing the job training program.

An output refers to the internal activities of a program (e.g., the products or services delivered). The output answers the question "What does the program do to achieve its goal or purpose?" For example, a job training program may provide a class to teach someone the skills necessary to find a job. An output measure may be the number of people who complete a job training program. Together, outcome, output, and efficiency measures should tell a comprehensive story of program performance. For more information, please see PART guidance pp. 6-10 and "Performance Measurement Challenges and Strategies" (http:///www.whitehouse.gov/omb/part/challenges_strategies.html).

---

[78] From PART FAQ's: http://www.whitehouse.gov/omb/part/2004_faq.html - 11

What is an acceptable efficiency measure?

An acceptable efficiency measure captures a program's ability to implement its activities and achieve results (an outcome or output), relative to resources (an input such as cost and/or time). The best kind of efficiency measure addresses the cost of achieving a unit of outcome. Efficiency measures must be useful, relevant to program purpose, and help improve program performance. (see PART Guidance, pp. 6-10 and for examples of efficiency measures, please see www.whitehouse.gov/omb/part/performance_measure_examples.pdf)

Do we have to have an efficiency measure for every program?

Yes, every program should have an efficiency measure or be in the process of developing one. Programs are required to have an annual efficiency measure to receive credit on the PART (question 2.3). Programs can receive credit for efficiency measures that are under development and may also receive credit for efficiency measures that are longer-term in scope. Although not required, programs are encouraged to develop outcome-based efficiency measures. (See PART guidance, pp. 6-10 and PART guidance on PART questions 2.1 and 2.3, pp. 18-22.)

The PART Guidance says that performance measures must be "meaningful." What does that mean?

A performance measure is "meaningful" if it measures the right thing – usually the outcome the program is intended to achieve. In assessing performance measures it is helpful to start with the definition of the program's purpose and the strategic goal(s) to which the program contributes. Performance measures should be relevant to the program, and therefore capture the most important aspects of a program's mission and priorities. Meaningful measures will be useful for the program partners, stakeholders, and citizens. Although it is tempting to design measures around existing data, those are not always the most meaningful.

To be considered "ambitious," is there a certain threshold a target must meet?

No. There is no standard threshold or percent increase that is required for a target to be considered "ambitious." Every program will be different given the context in which it operates and its current baseline. An "ambitious" target is one that promotes continued improvement, not just increases. For example, sometimes data collection for a program will indicate an increase in desired results due to demographic or other changes outside of the program. An ambitious target should strive for improved performance above and beyond these shifts. It is sometimes helpful to benchmark a program's targets against similar programs or against its own historical trends.

How can we set targets if we do not know what our future budgets will be?

Performance targets should be set assuming current budget level, allowing for reasonable changes in the future (where they can be anticipated). Agencies should not set targets that are not achievable given current program characteristics, or that would require significant increases in funding. It is anticipated that having good performance information will assist agencies in developing and justifying their budget requests. Agencies must be able to adjust their targets based on actual, enacted budgets.

APPENDIX B: ANALYTICAL HIERARCHY PROCESS

Decision-making often includes the weighing of multiple criteria, evaluation of trade-offs and coming to consensus as a group. The application of consistent scoring mechanisms can introduce subtle errors into analysis. The need to use both quantitative and qualitative information often characterizes real-world cases and distinguishes them from the simpler examples in textbooks. These features often lead to the implementation of some form of the Analytic Hierarchy Process (AHP). The fact that it succeeds in performing relative rankings and other complex tasks in a straightforward manner may explain why OMB suggests that such methods be used in decision-making.

AHP can be characterized as a multi-criteria decision technique in which qualitative factors are of prime importance. A model of the problem is developed using a hierarchical representation. That is, various sub-goals are generally specified that contribute to the top goal. At the top of the hierarchy is the overall goal or prime objective one is seeking to fulfill. The lower levels then represent the progressive decomposition of the problem. The knowledgeable parties (e.g., individual team members) complete a pair-wise comparison of all entries in each level relative to each of the entries in the next higher level of the hierarchy. The composition of these judgments fixes the relative priority of the entities at the lowest level (e.g., individual team members) relative to achieving the top-most objective.

This approach has been used in aviation safety applications, hazmat shipping evaluations,[79] and other related areas.

Software for AHP implementation includes commercial packages, such as Expert Choice 11 and ERGO 2001,[80] and it is straightforward to implement the process as a Microsoft Access® application or in a spreadsheet. The basic AHP calculations have been well documented in many publications and other sources.

---

[79] See, "Assessing the Impacts from the Introduction of Advanced Transport Telematics Technologies in Hazardous Materials Fleet Management", by K.G. Zografos and N. Androutsopoulos, Athens University of Economics and Business, Department of Management Science and Marketing, undated.

[80] See, http://www.expertchoice.com/software/, and www.arlingtonsoft.com, respectively.

APPENDIX C: VERBAL EXPRESSIONS OF PROBABILITY[81]

Verbal Expression	Numerical Range
Very small chance Poor chance	0-10
Small chance Doubtful	10-30
Perhaps May Chance not great	30-50
It could be	50
Likely Reasonable chance Reasonable to assume One could assume It seems It seems to me Can expect	50-70
High chance Close to certain	70-90
Very high chance Most likely	90-100

---

[81] See, Beyth-Marom.

APPENDIX D: THE DELPHI TECHNIQUE APPLIED TO CREATING POSSIBILITY DISTRIBUTIONS[82]

A natural approach for a group to build possibility distributions is to employ the Delphi technique. The Delphi technique is a process used to elicit information or judgments from participants through an iterative information exchange process. The participants in the Delphi process can be experts or stakeholders with a knowledge of or interest in the information being gathered.

Operationally, the Delphi technique does not require that the participants be co-located. The iterative information exchange process that is at the heart of the Delphi technique can be accomplished in person, through virtual meetings, or in written form.

A team or individual functioning as a coordinator manages the Delphi process. The coordinator creates an initial questionnaire, which is then sent to all participants. The responses are collected and reviewed by the coordinator. Based on those responses, a new questionnaire is developed and sent to all of the participants. The process continues with additional questionnaires that are always based on the results of the questionnaire until consensus is achieved. If consensus cannot be achieved (or if consensus is not the goal), the coordinator can achieve resolution in a variety of ways, including voting. To help ensure the true opinions of all participants are obtained, all responses are confidential.

The general theme of the questions remains the same in each subsequent questionnaire. For instance, an initial questionnaire might be sent to port security officers asking the general question "What are effective methods of physical security at ports?" The first questionnaire would be open ended and participants would be expected to list the methods that they consider effective. The second questionnaire might list the methods submitted and ask for comments concerning the strengths and weaknesses of each, while still encouraging additional methods to be submitted. A third questionnaire might include summarized responses from the second. After the third, the coordinator might send out a request to rank the methods according to their relative effectiveness. The coordinator would then send out a summary of the "vote", allowing participants to benefit from shared knowledge among colleagues about various physical security techniques, while the coordinator obtains data for further analysis or modeling.

While the Delphi technique can be very effective, it can also fail for a number of reasons. Those include:

- Imposing the coordinator's opinions or preconceptions on the process
- Ignoring and not exploring disagreements that arise in the responses
- Failing to properly summarize and present the responses
- Failing to choose a proper group for exploring the question of interest

---

[82] This section follows the discussion of the Delphi method the previous report in this series, Volpe National Transportation Systems Center (b).

The last problem can arise in any situation, of course, and is not limited necessarily to the Delphi technique. Because the development of possibility curves has a natural appeal, with its emphasis on a linguistic approach and a comparative lack of the restrictions, it is likely to be easier to apply Delphi methods and develop consistent possibility distributions.

BIBLIOGRAPHY

Ackerman, Gary et al., *Literature Review of Existing Terrorist Behavior Modeling*, The Center for Nonproliferation Studies, Monterey Institute of International Studies, August, 2002.

Almog, Doron, "Cumulative Deterrence and the War on Terrorism," *Parameters*, Winter 2004-05, pp. 4-19.

Armantier, Olivier, *Estimates of own Lethal Risks and Anchoring Effects*, manuscript, Department of Economics, University of Montreal, August 2005.

Beyth-Marom, Ruth, "How Probable is Probable? A Numerical Translation of Verbal Probability Expressions," *Journal of Forecasting*, Vol 1, 1982, pp. 257-269.

Chapman, Robert and Chi Leng, *Cost-Effective Responses to Terrorist Risks in Constructed Facilities*, National Institute of Standards and Technology, US Department of Commerce, NISTIR 7073, March, 2004.

Darby, John
    (a), *Evaluating Terrorist Risk Using Possibility Theory*, Los Alamos National Laboratory, LA-UR-04-0904, undated.

    (b), *Evaluating Terrorist Risk with Possibility Theory*, Los Alamos National Laboratory, LA-14179, November 2004.

Davis, Paul and Brian Michael Jenkins, *Deterrence & Influence in Counterterrorism: A Component in the War on al Qaeda*, RAND National Defense Research Institute, 2002.

Di Tella, Rafael and Ernesto Schargrodsky, *Using a Terrorist Attack to Estimate the Effect of Police on Crime*, Draft working paper, Harvard University and Universidad Torcuado Di Tella, respectively, February 2002.

Dubois, Didier, "Possibility Theory and Statistical Reasoning," *Computational Statistics & Data Analysis*, Elsevier Articles in Press, 2006.

Dubios, Didier, Henri Prade, and Phillipe Smets, "New Semantics for Quantitative Possibility Theory," *2nd International Symposium on Imprecise Probabilities and Their Applications*, Ithaca, New York, 2001.

Goertzel, Ted, *Econometrics as Junk Science*, Rutgers University, monograph; expanded form of article published in *The Skeptical Inquirer*, Vol 26:1, January/February 2002, pp. 19-23.

Harrald, John, Hugh Stephens and Johann Rene vanDorp, "A Framework for Sustainable Port Security," *Journal of Homeland Security and Emergency Management*, Vol 1:2, 2004.

Honea, Bob, "U.S. Military Preparedness – Jammed in the Traffic?," TR News 211, November-December 2000, pp. 18-24.

Huang, Bo, Cheu Ruey Long and Yong Seng Liew, "GIS-AHP Model for HAZMAT Routing with Security Considerations," *IEEE 6th International Conference on Intelligent Transporttaion Systems*, October, 2003.

Kardes, Erim and Randolph Hall, *Survey of Literature on Strategic Decision Making in the Presence of Adversaries*, CREATE Homeland Security Center, University of Southern California, March, 2005.

Kikuchi, Shinya and Partha Chakroborty, "Place of Possibility Theory in Transportation Analysis," *Transportation Research: Part B*, Vol 40, 2006, pp. 595-615.

Kuhn, Kenneth and Samer Madanat, "Model Uncertainty and the Management of a System of Infrastructure Facilities," *Transportation Research: Part C*, Vol 13, 2005, pp. 391-404.

Layne, Mary et al., "Appendix C: Prior Research," *Measuring the Deterrent Effect of Enforcement Operations on Drug Smuggling, 1991-1999*, Office of National Drug Control Policy, Available at: www.whitehousedrugpolicy.gov/publications/enforce/measure_effect_2001, March 2002.

Liesio, Juuso, Pekka Mild and Ahti Salo, "Preference Programming for Robust Portfolio Modeling and Project Selection," *European Journal of Operational Research*, Articles in Press, 2006.

Liu, Hua-Wen and Gou-Jun Wang, "Multi-Criteria Decision Making Methods Based on Intuitionistic Fuzzy Sets," *European Journal of Operational Research*, Articles in Press, 2006.

Maritime Transport Committee, *Security in Maritime Transport: Risk Factors and Economic Impact*, Organization for Economic Co-operation and Development, July 2003.

Markram, Bianca, "Terrorism Modelling: An Insoluble Problem?," *Reactions*, July 2002, pp. 24-30.

Morgan, M. Granger and Max Henrion, *Uncertainty: A Guide to Dealing with Uncertainty in Quantitative Risk and Policy Analysis*, Cambridge University Press, 1990.

MSRAM Training & Software Manual, undated.

Perl, Raphael, *Combating Terrorism: The Challenge of Measuring Effectiveness*, Congressional Research Service, The Library of Congress, November, 2005.

Quirk, Michaela and Steven Fernandez, "Infrastructure Robustness for Multiscale Critical Missions," *Journal of Homeland Security and Emergency Management*, Vol 2:2, 2005.

Raufaste, Eric, Rui da Silva Neves, and Claudette Marine, "Testing the Descriptive Validity of Possibility Theory in Human Judgments of Uncertainty," *Artificial Intelligence*," preprint.

Risk Management Solutions, Inc.,
    (a) *A Risk-Based Rationale for Extending the Terrorism Risk Insurance Act*, Newark, CA, 2005.

    (b) *Managing Terrorism Risk*, available at www.rms.com, 2003.

US Government Accountability Office, *Risk Management: Further Refinements Needed to Assess Risk and Prioritize Protective Measures at Ports and Other Critical Infrastructure*, GAO-06-91, December 2005.

Viscusi, Kip and William Evans, "Behavioral probabilities," *Journal of Risk & Uncertainty*, Vol 32, 2006, pp. 5-15.

Willis, Henry and David Ortiz, *Evaluating the Security of the Global Containerized Supply Chain*, Technical report, RAND Corporation, 2004.

Willis, Henry et al., *Estimating Terrorism Risk*, RAND Corporation, 2005.

Woo, Gordon, "Benefit-Cost Analyses for Malevolent Human Actions," Note prepared for the *Columbia/Penn Roundtable*, April, 2002.

Xue, Yifei and Donald Brown, "Spatial Analysis with Preference Specification of Latent Decision Makers for Criminal Event Prediction," *Decision Support Systems*, Vol 41, 2006, pp. 560-573.

Volpe National Transportation Systems Center,
    (a) *Port & Maritime Security Law Review*, Final Draft, December 2005.

    (b) *Port Security Metrics: Performance Measure Model Options*, Final Draft, January 2006.

www.ingramcontent.com/pod-product-compliance
Lightning Source LLC
Chambersburg PA
CBHW081903170526
45167CB00007B/3130